PRAISE FOR *FATAL FORECAST*

"Tougias spins a marvelous and terrifying yarn. . . . This is a breath-taking book."

—*Los Angeles Times*

"Ernie Hazard's experience, as related by Tougias, deserves a place as a classic of survival at sea."

—*The Boston Globe*

"Tougias's terrifying tale will stun you . . . leaving you breathless, exhilarated, and finally amazed. [He] knows how to spin a yarn—when to break away from heart-pounding action and when to keep it at a fever pitch. No wonder his previous book *Ten Hours Until Dawn* was selected one of the top books of the year."

—*The Providence Journal*

"A story like this is going to draw comparisons with the gold standard of sinking trawler tales, *The Perfect Storm,* and it proves itself a worthy, if slightly more uplifting, heir to its predecessor. This page-turner puts readers in the pilothouse with some rugged anglers."

—*Boston* magazine

"A Top Pick for Summer Reading."

—*Chicago Tribune*

"Tougias smartly leavens his spare narrative with similar worst-case scenarios that resulted when other seamen miscalculated the sea's wrathful power. . . . Practically a how-to lesson in high seas survival skills."

—*Publishers Weekly*

"A passionately recounted peril-at-sea adventure described with excruciating intensity. *Fatal Forecast* is a seafarer's delight, rendered with gusto."

—*Kirkus Reviews*

"A meticulously researched and vividly told true story that is by turns tragic, thrilling, and inspiring."

—*The Nantucket Independent*

"Tougias brings us through the harrowing tale deftly. . . . One can cherish an awe-inspiring miracle ending."

—*North Shore Sunday*

PRAISE FOR *TEN HOURS UNTIL DAWN*

"Arguably the best story of peril at sea since Sebastian Junger's *The Perfect Storm*."

—*Booklist* (starred review)

"Tougias delivers a well-researched, vividly written tale of brave men overwhelmed by the awesome forces of nature."

—*Publishers Weekly*

ALSO BY MICHAEL J. TOUGIAS

The Finest Hours:
The True Story of the U.S. Coast Guard's Most Daring Sea Rescue
(coauthor Casey Sherman)

Ten Hours Until Dawn:
The True Story of Heroism and Tragedy Aboard the *Can Do*

Until I Have No Country:
A Novel of King Philip's Indian War

River Days:
Exploring the Connecticut River from Source to Sea

King Philip's War
(coauthor Eric Schultz)

Quabbin: A History and Explorers' Guide

The Blizzard of '78

AMC's Best Day Hikes Near Boston

Nature Walks in Central and Western Massachusetts
(coauthor Rene Laubach)

There's a Porcupine in My Outhouse:
Misadventures of a Mountain Man Wannabe

FATAL FORECAST

AN INCREDIBLE TRUE TALE OF DISASTER
AND SURVIVAL AT SEA

MICHAEL J. TOUGIAS

Scribner

NEW YORK   LONDON   TORONTO   SYDNEY

Scribner
A Division of Simon & Schuster, Inc.
1230 Avenue of the Americas
New York, NY 10020

First Scribner trade paperback edition June 2009

SCRIBNER and design are registered trademarks of The Gale Group, Inc., used under
license by Simon & Schuster, Inc., the publisher of this work.

For information about special discounts for bulk purchases, please contact Simon &
Schuster Special Sales at 1-866-506-1949 or business@simonandschuster.com.

The Simon & Schuster Speakers Bureau can bring authors to your live event. For more
information or to book an event contact the Simon & Schuster Speakers Bureau at
1-866-248-3049 or visit our website at www.simonspeakers.com.

Designed by Kyoko Watanabe

Manufactured in the United States of America

8   10   9   7

Library of Congress Cataloging-in-Publication Data is available.

ISBN 978-0-7432-9703-5
ISBN 978-0-7432-9704-2 (pbk)
ISBN 978-1-4165-4644-3 (ebook)

To THE CREWS OF THE
FAIR WIND, SEA FEVER, AND *BROADBILL*

Dave Berry
Brad Bowen
Gary Brown
Peter Brown
Billy Garnos
Ernie Hazard
Grant Moore
Richard Rowell
Rob Thayer

CONTENTS

CONTENTS

PROLOGUE

GEORGES BANK, LOCATED ONE HUNDRED MILES EAST of Cape Cod, Massachusetts, is one of the richest fishing grounds in the world. It is an oval-shaped plateau on the ocean's floor, roughly the size of Massachusetts, Rhode Island, and Connecticut combined. Sixteen thousand years ago, during the ice age, Georges Bank was land, not sea, a broad coastal plain connected to the rest of North America. Nearby Nantucket and Martha's Vineyard were the largest hills in the region. As the glaciers melted and retreated, water filled in the deeper channels around Georges Bank, making it an island. Trapped on this enormous island of pine, juniper, and oak were land animals such as woolly mammoths, mastodons, moose, and caribou, whose teeth are today sometimes brought up in fishing nets. As the sea rose, more of the island flooded, and roughly six thousand years ago all of it was submerged.

Water depths on Georges Bank are irregular; in some places canyons plunge thousands of feet deep, while in other sections shoals of sand rise to within ten feet of the ocean's surface. Such shallow waters have led to exaggerated tales of fishermen claiming to have played baseball in ankle-deep water during low tide. The shoals are the very reason fishermen venture onto the Bank. Rays of sunlight can reach the bottom, allowing plankton to grow. Small fish gather to feed on the plankton and larger fish in turn prey on them.

The Bank's tremendous currents also contribute to the fishery by creating a high-energy environment of cycling nutrients and oxygen, but these currents, a swirling combination of tidal and surface waves, produce a constant turbulence when they collide over the sandy shoals. Many of the first fishermen to visit the Bank never went back, fearing the currents were too strong for them to safely anchor their boats. One early fisherman recounted a grim story of what happens when an anchor cable snaps. He was on board an anchored vessel in a storm when another boat, whose anchor had broken loose, careened past his boat. "The drifting vessel was coming directly at us. . . . With the swiftness of a gull she passed by, so near that I could have leapt aboard. The hopeless, terror-stricken faces of the crew we saw but a moment." The doomed ship then struck another vessel and both went down. The Georges Bank fisherman closed his observation by writing, "We knew that many a poor fellow who had left Gloucester full of hope, would never more return."

Georges Bank is also dangerous because of its location in the Atlantic. On the eastern end of the Bank the warm waters of the Gulf Stream collide with the cold Labrador Current, creating swirling waves. Although the currents at Georges Bank are almost always rough, when strong winds are added, chaotic seas occur, particularly in the shoal waters where vicious waves suddenly crest and break. Fishermen who venture out to Georges Bank need a boat large and sturdy enough to handle these seas. Here, help, should you need it, is hours away, an eternity if your vessel is going down. Captains fishing Georges Bank understand this, and the smart ones keep their boats in tip-top shape and always have one ear glued to the radio, listening to each and every updated weather report. If a big storm is coming, they get out of its way—fast.

The floor of the Bank is littered with rotted, rusting wrecks, and today's draggers must dodge them or risk snagging their nets. Some wrecks have been identified, but most are unknown. Year upon year, boats have a way of disappearing on Georges Bank. Even with radios, many vessels that sink give no indication of their coming doom. Something sudden and catastrophic happens, and the boat sinks within seconds, joining the hundreds of others on the bottom.

The deadly nature of Georges Bank is the trade-off fishermen must reckon with to get at catches richer than those found closer to shore. To fish the Bank one must accept the risk. This is not an environment for the fainthearted. The men who work the Bank are a rugged lot, who quickly develop a certain toughness that keeps fear in check. One of these men was thirty-three-year-old Ernie Hazard. What he endured on Georges Bank is nothing short of remarkable.

PART I

PART 1

CHAPTER 1

The *Fair Wind* Crew

ERNIE HAZARD WAS IN HIS THIRD YEAR OF OFF-shore lobster fishing, and although the work was brutally demanding, he felt fortunate. The *Fair Wind,* a 50-foot steel lobster boat on which Ernie worked, was a meticulously maintained vessel equipped with the most modern gear and electronics. Equally important, Ernie enjoyed the company of his fellow crewmembers and his captain—no one slacked off and everyone contributed to making the *Fair Wind* a very profitable boat.

On November 20, 1980, the crew was having dinner at the Backside Saloon in Hyannis, Massachusetts, enjoying a good meal before making the last trip of the season. The men had made close to thirty fishing trips to Georges Bank since the previous April, and they were all looking forward to having the next four months off. Ernie talked about going down to Florida to see his brother or possibly heading out to Carmel, California, to visit friends. Thirty-year-old captain Billy Garnos planned to focus on his new house and his fiancée. Rob Thayer, age twenty-two, hadn't made any definite plans, but he hoped to travel, having spent prior off-seasons in such far-flung places as Labrador and Newfoundland. Dave Berry, the youngest crewmember at just twenty years old, lived up in Marblehead, Massachusetts, and he'd likely take a little time off to be with friends before working at his father's wholesale fish business.

Ernie felt relaxed that night, quietly listening as the rest of the crew discussed their plans. Every now and then he made a joke or a wry comment. The others had come to enjoy his self-deprecating humor and quick, dry wit. They also appreciated the muscle and stamina packed into his burly six-foot frame. He had arms as big as most men's thighs, and he put those arms to good use hauling and setting lobster traps. He looked tough and perhaps a bit menacing with his muscular arms, piercing black eyes, and wild black beard, but his crewmates knew that behind the gruff exterior was an intelligent and thoughtful man.

But Ernie was no saint, and occasionally he and Billy Garnos would pound down a few rounds of beers after a week at sea and raise a little hell. This was especially true after they'd managed to harpoon a swordfish in addition to catching lobster, when each had a wad of cash in his pocket. Neither man went looking for trouble, but some situations called for Ernie to throw a punch or two. After most trips, however, all Ernie really wanted to do was rest for a couple of days before heading back out to Georges Bank and the bone-numbing work of lobstering.

Although Ernie, at age thirty-three, was the oldest of the crew, the others had been fishing just as long or longer. Ernie got his position on board the *Fair Wind* by simply answering a help wanted advertisement he'd seen in the newspaper three years earlier. He was single and living in Peabody, Massachusetts, bouncing from one factory job to another, making lightbulbs at the General Electric plant in Lynn and working for a concrete manufacturer. When Ernie saw the advertisement for a crewman, he was between jobs, so he figured, What the heck, that's something I've never done.

The boat's owner, Charlie Raymond, worked alongside Billy Garnos and another crew member, so Ernie became the fourth crewman. Ernie had never been offshore, and on his first trip out he couldn't help but think that he had entered another world as he gazed at the gray ocean stretching endlessly in all directions. Some newcomers to commercial fishing get spooked and disoriented on their initial voyage when they realize how insignificant their boat is compared to the enormous seas. But Ernie was fascinated by the new experience, and Charlie Raymond and Billy Garnos kept him busy from the moment he set foot on the *Fair Wind,* teaching him everything they could. "They had me driving the boat," says Ernie, "which was a big deal for me. I'd never driven a fifty-foot boat, and I loved every minute of it. Plowing through that vast open space was a thrill, and I remember thinking this is absolutely incredible—it was all so new and different."

Ernie's initial trip on the *Fair Wind* was also the boat's first of the season. When they reached the fishing grounds after a twenty-hour ride, Ernie learned what it took to make a living from the sea. "I wondered how long these people were going to work without taking a rest," says Ernie. "They seemed tireless." The boat was loaded with dozens of traps, and they had to bait each one and then drop it down. There were twenty-two traps to a trawl (a set or string of traps), and on that trip they dropped three trawls, working throughout the day and well into the night.

As backbreaking as the work seemed, the next trip was even tougher. The crew had to haul in the previously set traps, rebait them, then drop them over again. Ernie's hands had not yet developed calluses, and his tender flesh was in constant pain from pulling so much rope. He found he had muscles in his hands and forearms that he'd never felt before, and they ached incessantly. But he didn't complain. He already knew that this work was more rewarding than his manufacturing jobs. It paid better too, but that didn't matter to him; the satisfaction was in the work itself, the ocean setting, and the guys who worked beside him.

The trips fell into a pattern of five days out at sea, and then a day or two back in port. Ernie's skin quickly developed thick calluses, and the muscles in his hands became so large he could barely touch his thumb to his smallest finger. Charlie and Billy continued to teach him about the boat and lobstering, and Ernie soaked up as much as he could, enthralled by this new ocean world. Each trip was different; sometimes the North Atlantic unleashed an angry series of pounding waves, but other times the water remained as smooth as glass, and the crew could tell the difference between a swordfish and a shark from the surface almost a mile away.

Ernie's pay depended on the catch, and his cut of the boat's profits was slightly lower than those of the more senior men. When the catch was poor, all the crew suffered. "If we weren't catching lobster," says Ernie, "the work just seemed like ballbusting labor. But when we had good days, there was no feeling quite like it. It wasn't just that we would make more money, but more a feeling that 'we did it.' And we never knew how many lobster we would haul up or what else would be in the trap." On one trip the only thing caught in the trap was a lobster claw, but what a claw it was. It measured seventeen inches long and contained fifteen pounds of meat. Ernie kept the claw, removed the meat, lacquered the shell, and mounted it at his mother's home to show friends who couldn't believe its size. The lobster from which the claw had come likely measured five feet from the tail to the outstretched claw.

Over the course of the season, as Ernie got to know Charlie and Billy, he began to view them as a family and he understood how each man relied on the other. A crewmate's energy and natural disposition become apparent within a couple days, and he either gels with the rest of the crew or he doesn't. Everything becomes magnified in this self-contained world, and if someone isn't pulling his weight or can't fit in with the men already on board, he doesn't stay long. This kind of crewmember can poison a boat and its productivity.

For the three years Ernie fished on the *Fair Wind* he was lucky to work with great crewmembers, and because the boat was successful, there was very little turnover. During Ernie's second year, owner Charlie Raymond made Billy Garnos the captain so that Charlie could concentrate on the construction of a bigger boat and focus on the business needs of his growing fleet. Billy, an unusually generous young man who had bought a home and invited his parents and grandmother to live with him and who was now saving for a second home for himself and his fiancée, proved an able skipper. Charlie promised Billy that when the bigger boat was ready, it would be his to captain.

Billy came by his interest in the sea from the surf-casting he used to do with his father growing up. Billy and neighborhood pal Frank Sholds would climb into Mr. Garnos's ancient truck and the three of them would drive from their hometown of Beverly, Massachusetts, up to Plum Island near the New Hampshire border for some striper fishing. Years later, it was Frank who first tried his hand at commercial fishing for offshore lobsters. Billy, fresh from a tour of duty in Vietnam and working at a local supermarket, was impressed with Frank's big paychecks and soon followed in his friend's footsteps. Through Frank, Billy met Charlie Raymond and became a deckhand on the *Fair Wind*. Billy made up for his inexperience with his strong back, quick mind, and good work ethic, and he labored on the boat in whatever capacity was needed, from cook to engineer. Unlike some commercial fishermen who blew half their weekly checks the first day they were back in port, Billy saved a good portion of his. It was this maturity and sense of loyalty that caught the eye of

Charlie Raymond, and Charlie knew he had just the kind of man he wanted to captain his boat.

Rob Thayer and Dave Berry rounded out the rest of the crew, and all of them had great respect and confidence in Billy as their captain. The four men had formed a tight bond, and they often chose to have dinner together before setting back out to sea. For Rob Thayer, this was his first season aboard the *Fair Wind,* but after the steep learning curve of the first few weeks, he was now pulling his weight just like the others. Rob and Dave Berry, both in their early twenties, formed a quick friendship. Dave was an experienced deckhand, having worked on the ocean since he was fifteen. He too saved a good deal of his fishing pay and had just bought a new pickup truck, which he paid off in no time. A little of Billy Garnos's sense of responsibility and maturity may have rubbed off on Dave because just before the year-end trip to Georges Bank he treated his mother to lunch and talked with her about investing his money. He also visited his father and indicated that after the trip he'd like to try working in his dad's wholesale fish business with an eye toward becoming a partner someday.

Young, confident, and hardworking, the crew seemingly had their whole lives in front of them.

Now, as the four men ate and talked at the Backside Saloon, they knew the upcoming week at Georges Bank would be a cold one. Late-November temperatures could be expected to hover in the 40s and 50s during the day and drop lower at night. Still, the more important factors were the wind, and whether or not storms were forecast for the region. Whenever Billy learned of an approaching storm before a late-season trip, he'd delay departure until the storm passed. Georges Bank in November could be a very nasty place, and it was not the time of year to take chances.

The next morning, the men met at sunrise and prepared the

boat for the final trip, stowing food, bait, and gear. The old fisherman's superstition that it's bad luck to leave on a Friday did not deter the crew and never had. Men like Ernie and Billy felt that if you put stock in superstitions you'd never get any fishing done. The crew of the *Fair Wind* felt no sense of foreboding that day, no ominous premonitions.

As he'd done the night before, Billy listened to the National Weather Service forecast for Georges Bank. The forecast called for southeast winds of 15 to 25 knots, shifting to northwest at 20 to 30 knots at night, followed by similar conditions for Saturday with some rain and fog. Seas would be three to six feet Friday and five to ten feet on Saturday. The report was quite typical for Georges Bank, and the crew of the *Fair Wind* had no reason to doubt its accuracy.

One of the key components of forecasting weather at sea is the information obtained from weather buoys. The weather buoys transmit hourly reports on sea-level pressure, air temperature, sea surface temperature, wave height, and the all-important wind speed and direction. On that day, however, the Georges Bank buoy was malfunctioning. And just to the north, the Gulf of Maine buoy was not even afloat, but was on land being repaired. Thus, the weather report was based on incomplete data. The management at the National Weather Service, which is part of the National Oceanic and Atmospheric Administration (NOAA), had known about the situation for months, but they had elected not to alert mariners of the problem.

Billy Garnos, Ernie Hazard, Rob Thayer, and Dave Berry headed out to sea based on what they believed to be the same reliable forecasts they had grown to trust over the years. They looked forward to a smooth trip.

But on that November day, the *Fair Wind* was on a collision course with a storm that produced waves more monstrous than anything the crew had ever seen.

CHAPTER 2

Heading Out

ERNIE HAZARD GREW UP IN COCHITUATE, MASSA-chusetts, located about twenty miles west of Boston. Although he didn't spend much time near the ocean, he loved the water, particularly Dudley Pond and nearby swamps. He and his brothers would spend hours on end fishing for horned pout and pickerel, catching frogs and turtles, but mostly just wandering around the woods and wetlands the way kids did back in the time before computers, PlayStation, and cable TV.

Ernie's father died when he was fifteen, and Ernie, who was already independent-minded and stubborn, spent more time in the swamps and less time at school. At the beginning of his senior year his mother remarried and she and her husband relocated to Peabody, but Ernie refused to go. Instead he got a job at a gas station near Cochituate, and continued at school during the day and pumped gas in the evening. At night he slept inside the garage of the gas station. When school officials discovered this, they forced him out of school because he didn't have a parent living in the town, and Ernie reluctantly joined his mother in Peabody.

Just before graduation from high school, he was drafted and entered the army in November. He was trained in mechanics and within a few months found himself serving in Korea. One would think that a freewheeling teenager would rebel against army life, but Ernie didn't mind the rigors of the service, and he loved the experience of traveling overseas. When his hitch was up he returned to Peabody and landed a job at the nearby General Electric plant. Most of the money he made went into his passions—motorcycles and good times. Like many young men, he drifted around, hungry for new experiences, feeling as if he could do anything. The difference between Ernie and most other young men was that Ernie didn't just talk about adventure, he went out and found it. He once took a year off from working to tour the West Coast. Determined not to be a passive tourist, he decided to travel the back roads, under his own power, and alone. He hitchhiked to Washington State, bought a bicycle, and pedaled south on a three-month odyssey. He didn't stop until he reached Mexico.

When Ernie joined the crew of the *Fair Wind,* he bonded quickly with his crewmates because in many ways they were a lot like him: tough, independent, and willing to try new adventures. While friends were settling down in nine-to-five jobs, these men were out on the ocean from April through November, working eighteen-hour days. In those eight months at sea the goal was simple: make as much money as possible so that during the winter months they could do whatever they pleased.

This freedom was made possible by a bottom-dwelling crustacean with a greenish-brown shell, the lobster. These ancient, armored creatures have two huge specialized claws. The right one acts as a pincher, and the slightly larger left claw is used as a crusher. With these powerful tools lobsters catch and crush both living and dead organisms, including fish, sea worms, mollusks, and small crustaceans. They are also cannibalistic, attacking smaller members of their own species. As a lobster ages, it outgrows the limits of its shell and must molt, or "shed," by splitting its shell and wriggling free. For the next several days the lobster is soft and vulnerable, and when predators approach, the lobster's only defense is to hide among rocks until its new shell hardens.

Lobster habitat is often found in shallow, craggy coastal areas, but these creatures can also live in depths of up to four hundred fathoms and are particularly abundant in the submarine canyons of Georges Bank. These offshore lobsters travel more extensively than their coastal cousins, often covering as many as 180 miles during spring migrations.

Prior to the 1950s, offshore lobsters were usually incidental catches in nets intended for other fish. Fishermen knew there were plenty of lobsters in the canyons and in the holes of the canyon walls, but conventional traps and nets were inefficient at capturing them. In the late 1950s, however, technological advances in trap design and hauling allowed fishermen to work the deep waters of Georges Bank, and the harvest of lobsters there increased fourfold between 1960 and 1969. Georges Bank lobsters were also considerably larger than those found inshore, with some reaching twenty pounds or more. But word spread quickly, attracting more boats to the Bank, and by the mid-1970s most of the big lobsters had been harvested, and the overall population had been significantly reduced. Despite the decline in catches, offshore lobstering still brought better yields than inshore, and boats like the *Fair Wind* found less competition from other lobstermen when they were out as far as Georges Bank. The bigger paydays, however, were not without a commensurate risk: should trouble strike, aid could be a long way off.

The crew of the *Fair Wind* used large wooden traps, each weighing about 125 pounds. Each of the twenty-two traps in a trawl were connected together with a polypropylene ground line, and the traps were spaced so that the entire trawl stretched for about a mile. The traps were then set with the prevailing current so there would be no slack in the line and they didn't get snarled, or "balled up." The first and the last traps on the trawl were weighted down with "end weights" to keep them anchored in place. These end traps were also connected to two large floating balls and a triangular radar reflector known as a high-flyer, which bobbed upright on the ocean's surface so that a boat's radar could home in on it. When the traps were lifted, the crewmen removed the lobsters, keeping the legal ones and throwing those that were undersized back into the sea. The crewmen took turns banding the lobsters and either rebaiting and lowering the traps or stacking them for placement in another area. Each man was lifting, sliding, and slinging tons of gear in a single day, and stacking the traps in rough seas was perhaps the most difficult of all the duties.

Working with heavy, cumbersome gear on a moving deck takes strength and athleticism, but endurance was, and still is, the primary attribute needed in a lobster fisherman. Every offshore boat aims to maximize its catch in as little time as possible. The goal of the *Fair Wind*'s crew was to get on and off the fishing grounds as quickly as possible, so the men put in seventeen to twenty hours each day.

As the *Fair Wind* left Hyannis around noon on Friday, November 21, the crew took two-hour shifts at the wheel. Driving the boat to the fishing grounds was the least demanding part of the trip, consisting of looking out the window for other boats and watching the radar. Dave Berry manned the wheel for the first couple of hours, glancing at the green glowing screen of the radar. The central point on the screen was the *Fair Wind*'s position, and from that center an electronic line ran clockwise around

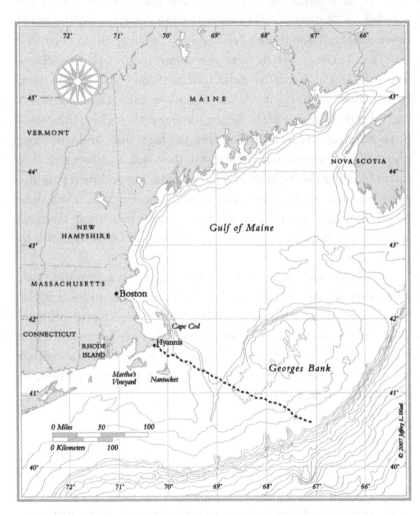

The dotted line indicates the approximate path the *Fair Wind* took on Friday, November 21, 1980, from Hyannis, Massachusetts, to the fishing grounds on Georges Bank.

the screen, highlighting any objects that fell within the radar's range. Usually the screen was blank, but every now and then a dot would appear, indicating another fishing boat, tanker, or freighter. The *Fair Wind*'s course had already been plotted with an electronic navigation aid called LORAN, so piloting the boat was just a matter of staying on course and leaving a wide berth between their boat and other vessels. Because the work was monotonous, shifts at the wheel were short. With the motion of the long swells of the open ocean and the droning of the *Fair Wind*'s 265-horsepower diesel engine, it was easy to get lulled to sleep.

Occasionally Dave raised another fishing vessel on the radio, both to keep himself alert and to check on the other boat's progress. On this trip, the nearest vessel was the *Sea Fever,* another commercial lobster boat also heading to Georges Bank for a season-ending trip. The two vessels floated five miles apart. Because they had worked in close proximity all summer, the crews were familiar with one another and glad to have a friendly boat nearby should any trouble arise. Both crews had a healthy respect for the ocean and knew that an unforeseen accident could pay a visit at any moment. Just four weeks earlier six crewmen aboard the 77-foot New Bedford trawler *Irene and Hilda* had been lost at sea when a storm capsized their boat.

Captained by William Rebello Sr., the *Irene and Hilda* had a deck crew of five men, one of whom was the captain's son John. On Saturday, October 25, the steel-hulled trawler was fifteen miles east of Nantucket heading to Georges Bank when it encountered twenty-foot waves and 60-knot winds. Although the boat was handling well and in no immediate trouble, Captain Rebello, who had twenty-five years of commercial fishing experience, decided to play it safe and return to port in New Bedford. Son John Rebello radioed his mother and told her they were aborting their trip because of the stormy conditions. Mrs. Rebello reminded her son to be careful coming in, and John replied it would be slow going in the heavy seas. She asked what time they could be expected back in port, and John replied about 5 or 6 a.m. the next morning. She closed their conversation with a simple "God bless." That would be the last time Mrs. Rebello ever heard from her son or husband.

When the *Irene and Hilda* did not return on Sunday morning, Mrs. Rebello alerted the Coast Guard and a massive search was launched, using six aircraft and two cutters that began scouring an 11,000-square-mile area east of Nantucket. At the Coast Guard's rescue coordination center in Boston a computer operator punched in the tide, sea, and wind conditions to determine where the vessel, a life raft, or men in the water may have drifted. They assured Mrs. Rebello that if anything was still afloat they had a 90 percent chance of finding it.

On Monday a Coast Guard aircraft spotted barrels bobbing in the water, and on Tuesday it was determined that they were the same type as the ones on board the lost vessel. Finding the barrels gave hope to family members that the search was zeroing in on the correct drift line of the vessel or crew. The Coast Guard, however, knew that finding floating debris from the ship was not a good sign; it probably meant the ship had capsized and sunk. On Wednesday, approximately thirty miles east of Nantucket, a fishing boat found a life ring from the *Irene and Hilda,* adding to the evidence that something catastrophic had happened to the missing vessel. Three more days went by with no additional finds, and a week after the vessel was first reported missing the Coast Guard ended the search.

The crew of the *Fair Wind* was well aware that late-season trips to Georges Bank could be dangerous, but they also had great confidence in their boat. The six-year-old, twenty-seven-ton, green and white *Fair Wind* had proven itself in heavy seas on numerous trips and Billy Garnos remained calm and steady at the wheel when the ocean grew angry. But a solid boat and captain meant nothing in the face of the great storm that was about to hit them.

CHAPTER 3

The Forecast

ON FRIDAY AFTERNOON ERNIE TOOK HIS TURN AT the wheel and was again swept up by the sense of freedom and contentment he always felt when piloting the *Fair Wind* southeast toward the vast open space of the fishing grounds. Visibility was good, and the *Fair Wind* easily rose up and over the gentle five-foot swells as its bow smoothly parted the seas, a white wake trailing astern. With the sun low in the southwestern sky behind him, Ernie looked out over the platinum sea and felt that he was exactly where he should be, at the right place and the right time. After living in Cochituate, Peabody, South Korea, Salem, and California, Ernie knew that the *Fair Wind* and the wild, seemingly boundless world of the North Atlantic was just where he belonged at this stage in his life. He was healthy, single, and happy, with the personal freedom to do whatever he wanted with his young life.

At 4 p.m. Rob Thayer took the wheel as the *Fair Wind* passed through an area known as the Great Round Shoal, putting the island of Nantucket behind its stern. Rob paid close attention to the radar screen, as he would soon be crossing the shipping lanes that run north-northwest for inbound traffic to Boston Harbor and south-southeast for outgoing vessels. These lanes keep ships on course and off the nearby shoals. Between these two lanes is a mile-wide separation zone to allow a margin of error. Just four years earlier the giant oil tanker *Argo Merchant* strayed outside of the lanes and paid the price, sinking when it hit a shoal.

Crossing the lanes could be dangerous because of the amount of traffic that used them. A small boat like the *Fair Wind* wouldn't stand a chance against a tanker or a freighter, and many of the fishing vessels that have simply disappeared probably met their ends this way. Often the crew of the larger boat doesn't even realize that they've run over a smaller vessel, or worse, the ship's skipper pretends not to notice and continues onward. The only clue that later links the ship to the accident is a streak of paint from the smaller boat running along the ship's hull. (A ship's radar may not pick up a small boat at all, and even if it does, it's often too late to avoid the collision, as it can take more than a quarter mile for a large ship to make a turn and a full mile and a half to stop.)

On this day, the *Fair Wind* crossed the shipping lanes without incident and continued east toward Georges Bank. Though collisions were rare on Georges Bank, conflicts between vessels using different types of gear were not. Fixed gear such as long lines, gill nets, and lobster trap trawls were often fouled by draggers such as scallopers. These incidents raised the tempers of crews on both types of boats, as accidents wasted precious time while gear was untangled and repaired. But such a conflict was unlikely to happen so late in the season, when many fishing boats had already made their last trips. On this day in November, the *Fair Wind* would be one of only a handful of boats working an area larger than southern New England—all the more reason for the *Fair Wind* to maintain radio communication with the other boat headed out for lobster, the *Sea Fever*.

* * *

As Rob steered the boat he periodically checked the VHF radio for weather forecasts, and the reports continued to call for fair conditions. Later, as the *Fair Wind* traveled out of range of the VHF signals, the powerful single sideband radio would be used to monitor the weather. These reports were announced on a fixed schedule every six hours, with the next report due at 11 p.m.

While Rob manned the helm, Billy stayed below with the others sleeping or reading. Once on the Bank, Billy would be as busy as the rest of the crew, although he'd be at the wheel much of the time while Ernie, Rob, and Dave worked on deck retrieving traps dropped a week earlier. Because this was their last trip of the season, they'd be spending considerable time stacking traps and coiling line once the gear was hauled up and the lobsters were dropped in the saltwater tanks below. Little motion would be wasted, as each crewman knew exactly what was expected of him. By this time in the season they could anticipate their fellow crewmen's each and every movement.

By working as a group they would push one another to work far harder than if they were working alone. Billy would join them on deck whenever he could leave the wheelhouse, and he would keep the pace up by moving constantly, helping wherever there was a need. After the second or third day, the grueling labor would catch up with their endurance. Lifting gear, which one man might have done alone on the first day, may now require assistance, and the crew would increasingly depend on one another. This would also be the time crewmen needed to be a bit more deliberate to avoid slipping on deck or getting a leg or arm caught in a line. It's an unwritten rule that the whole crew remain on deck until the job at hand is completed. If a crewman on deck got hurt or caught in a dangerous situation, his very life might depend on immediate assistance from a fellow crewman. Without help a man entangled in a trapline could be yanked overboard in the blink of an eye. It would be a long way down to a watery grave before his crewmates even noticed he was missing.

In spite of the intensity of the work, complaining would be rare. The whole crew knew that the difference between a successful trip and an unsuccessful one had often been the simple determination to keep going, to ignore fatigue and pain. They also knew that four men was exactly the right number of hands for this size vessel: any more and their share of the profit would decrease, while any less would mean hauling fewer traps.

Now, however, the heavy work was still twelve hours away, and the crew was relaxed and rested. Billy Garnos took over for Rob on the wheel, and Rob went below and settled into his bunk as the *Fair Wind* cut through the seas on its southeastward course.

As the *Fair Wind* approached the halfway mark to Billy Garnos's preferred fishing grounds on the southeastern edge of Georges Bank, a sinister force was collecting itself to the south. A low-pressure system was taking shape, silently gathering strength off the Carolina coast. The weather service knew about this low-pressure system, and they predicted a northeastward trajectory that would take the storm toward Nova Scotia, well east of Georges Bank. The only effect of the storm forecast for Georges Bank was for a few showers and windy conditions on Saturday. But the storm had other plans.

Forecasting weather at sea in 1980 was more challenging than it is today and far more difficult than forecasting land-based weather. A land storm passes over several dozen monitoring stations manned by meteorologists with the latest technology, making it virtually impossible to surprise a region totally. An ocean storm, on the other hand, has far fewer monitors. A meteorologist must rely on satellite images, high-altitude atmosphere balloons, weather buoys, and reports from passing ships. Two of these four monitoring tools were not available on that November night; not only were two weather buoys broken, no ships crossed directly through the low-pressure system's path. At the time the third tool, satellite imagery, was not reliable, still unable to penetrate clearly the high atmospheric cloud cover.

The meteorologist in charge of the National Weather Service office in Boston, Rodney Winslow, was not comfortable predicting ocean weather with one arm tied behind his back. He had repeatedly warned his superiors about the broken buoy at Georges Bank, writing in one memo that "this buoy is extremely important to us. . . . It serves as one of the few reliable observation points in an area where a tremendous number of fishing vessels operate daily. . . . I urge every effort be made to bring and maintain these buoys on continuous operational status. Must we once again open ourselves to political repercussion because of the failure of an important piece of equipment?"

The weather buoy in question had begun to malfunction as early as the spring of 1980, when it simply stopped reporting. In early August, it was hit by a ship, causing further damage. At-sea repairs were made on August 11, but on September 6 the wind sensor failed. Winslow's request to have it repaired again was denied by managers at the National Oceanographic and Atmospheric Administration, which oversees both the National Weather Service and the marine weather buoys. NOAA was wrestling with budget limitations, and it decided to wait to repair the buoy until January, when a new, improved type of wind sensor would be ready to install.

Of course, Ernie, Billy, Rob, and Dave knew nothing about this. So far the trip out to the Bank had been smooth going, and when Billy listened to the 11 p.m. weather forecast he heard nothing new.

The *Fair Wind* steamed eastward, as long, gentle swells rolled beneath her hull.

CHAPTER 4

In the Monster's Grip

ERNIE WOKE FROM HIS SLEEP AT 6 A.M. AND KNEW immediately that something was wrong. The *Fair Wind* pitched violently and he could feel the boat shudder with each breaking wave. As he threw on a pair of pants and slid into his work boots, he wondered what the hell had happened to the predicted five- to ten-foot seas. In the wheelhouse he found Dave on the wheel and Billy and Rob standing beside him. Outside, clouds of white spray slammed the windshield as the *Fair Wind* lurched through heavy swells.

Billy looked at Ernie and said, "Can you believe this shit?"

Ernie glanced out the pilothouse windows and saw a twenty-foot wave advancing toward them. "It sure doesn't look like five- to ten-foot seas," said Ernie sarcastically. "What did the five a.m. report say?"

"The forecast changed. It called for a gale warning with wind of thirty to forty knots and seas eight to fourteen feet. Dave was on the wheel and he woke me when he heard that. When I got up here the wind was already pushing fifty knots and the seas were easily running fifteen to twenty feet. And it's getting worse by the minute."

The crew knew they were too far out to sea to do anything other than keep the *Fair Wind*'s bow pointed into the seas, maintain position, and take the beating. They wanted to avoid breaking seas on the stern, which could damage gear and bury the boat under tons of churning water. If the weather forecast was even remotely credible, they were now facing the worst that the storm had to give, and things would soon improve. The *Fair Wind* was on Georges Bank at its southeastern end, near Munson Canyon, just a few miles from the edge of the continental shelf.

Outside the wind roared and rain flew almost horizontally, the drops splattering the boat like shotgun pellets. Visibility shrank to just twenty-five to fifty feet and a low cloud cover hovered just above the ocean. The angry, breaking seas filled the air with churning, frothing foam, making it difficult to determine where the sea ended and the sky began. They would haul no traps today, but the crew hoped that if the storm quickly subsided they might be able to work on Sunday.

Billy had Dave position the boat so that it was headed directly into the wind with the waves striking a couple degrees to port, which was the side of the pilothouse made of welded steel. The doors to the pilothouse were on the starboard side and Billy didn't want them to take a beating. He was playing it safe, although he knew the *Fair Wind* was a rugged boat and could easily take the punishment the seas were throwing at her. Billy wasn't worried about the weather as much as he was angry about the forecast. Just seven hours earlier, the 11 p.m. forecast had called for favorable weather. Had he known the day before that a storm would hit the Bank today, he would have turned back and waited for the weather to clear. Now it was too late.

Billy raised the *Sea Fever* on the radio to see how they were making out. The captain of the *Sea Fever*, Peter Brown, had taken the same action as Billy, pointing their bow into the sea, taking wave after wave, waiting it out. Brown made it clear that he too was fuming mad that the weather forecast had been dead wrong. By the time the 5 a.m. forecast predicted a gale, his boat was already in its grip. He wondered how the weather service could have made such a dire mistake.

By 7 a.m. the seas had grown to twenty-five feet, and some barrels of bait had come loose on the *Fair Wind*'s deck, rolling from side to side and banging the rail. The barrels could damage the boat or be swept overboard, where a loose line could become tangled in the propeller. If a propeller stops spinning, a boat can no longer be steered, and in high seas the results can be fatal. Without propeller power the boat will soon be sideways, or "beam to," the waves, and rough seas can quickly roll the boat.

Ernie and Billy had no choice but to risk going out on deck to secure the barrels in spite of the danger. At any moment an ill-timed breaking wave might sweep them overboard. When they left the safety of the pilothouse, the force of the wind staggered them as if they'd been punched by an unseen fist. The wind was so strong it tore the tops off the waves. Yellow spindrift, with the consistency of shaving cream, raced through the air, blurring and stinging their eyes. The two men found it difficult to breathe, so thick was the air with foam and water, and they turned their heads away from the wind. Spray cascaded over the deck and streamed out from the scuppers, making for slippery footing. The cold rain pelted them like tiny stones stinging their skin as the two fought to keep their balance on the heaving deck. Through the roar of the wind and water they could hear the mast wires howling as the wind blasted past. Beyond the boat's railing there was an absence of color: all that was visible was the white and gray churning sea.

Fighting their way toward the stern, Ernie and Billy had the disconcerting view of the seas converging on the boat. They faced the stern, and when the *Fair Wind* climbed up a wave they were looking down into the trough, then as the boat crested the wave they were looking up, hearing the whine of the propeller, wondering if it was grabbing water or just whirling around in the foam. They worked hunched over and low to the deck, wrestling with the barrels being buffeted by the 50-mile-per-hour gusts. Slowly, working together, they shoved the barrels back into position and lashed them down. Then they began securing the other equipment, desperate to get all the work done now so they wouldn't have to come back out later.

At 8 a.m. Ernie took over the wheel, and an exhausted Dave Berry retreated below to try to get some rest. The seas had grown to thirty feet. Ernie had to give a little throttle to maintain headway up and over the waves. The *Fair Wind* responded but occasionally took green water—not merely spray, but the sea itself—over her bow before asserting herself. Neither Ernie nor Billy, who had ten years of experience fishing on the Bank, had ever seen waves build so rapidly. It seemed that each advancing wave was a bit bigger than the last.

By 9 a.m. the seas were thirty-five to forty feet, and the wind had increased yet again, to sustained speeds of 50 to 60 knots. Every now and then a gust would roar in at 70 knots, and those savage blasts seemed to probe the boat for weaknesses. Each time a particularly vicious wave slammed the bow, Ernie felt thankful the *Fair Wind*'s hull was made of steel. He kept telling himself it couldn't get any worse, but Billy wasn't taking any chances, and he decided to flood one of the lobster tanks to give the boat more weight for greater stability. The *Fair Wind* had three covered tanks on board, each running from side to side, and Billy flooded the central tank with seawater using the diesel pump. The tanks were perfect for stabilization, because each had a small free surface area and a diameter that progressively widened farther down toward the hull. Very little water could slosh around the top, but the water in the deeper part of the tank lowered the vessel's center of gravity, causing the *Fair Wind* to have less freeboard, or surface area, to be buffeted by the wind and waves. The flooded central tank extended the full breadth and depth of the vessel and had a volume of 193 cubic feet, approximately six tons of seawater.

Ernie felt the propeller bite a little better with the extra weight, but he couldn't allow himself to relax even the slightest bit, not with the height of the waves beginning to equal the length of the boat. He steered and powered the *Fair Wind* more by feel than sight, and did his best to keep the boat's bow facing into the oncoming waves to reduce the incredible pounding they hurled at him.

CHAPTER 5

Multiple Maydays

THE FACT THAT A VIOLENT STORM STRUCK GEORGES Bank in late November was not surprising. Statistically, July is the calmest month with the smoothest seas, and the potential for storms increases with each subsequent month up to January, which boasts the most treacherous seas of all. Low-pressure storm systems or extratropical storms typically come from the west across the Great Lakes or from the south and then barrel up the U.S. coastline, often gathering strength if they remain over the sea. Writer Richard Backus, an expert on Georges Bank, reports that the storms that originate south of Georges Bank sometimes "show a phenomenon called 'explosive cyclogenesis' in which the storm deepens rapidly as cold, continental air strikes the warm water in or near the Gulf Stream. In some of these storms the barometric pressure has fallen as much as a millibar per hour for 24 hours." In other words, the low-pressure system literally blows up, becoming a winter hurricane. Making matters worse, these storms sometimes move with great speed, follow an erratic path, and join forces with other low-pressure systems. The storm exploding on Georges Bank was marked by all three of these characteristics, and its most intense winds were on the southeast side of the Bank, where the *Fair Wind* crew was engaged in the fight of their lives.

Although Georges Bank suffered the brunt of the storm, the storm threatened mariners up and down the New England coast, and the Coast Guard's worst nightmare was well under way. As early as 4:30 that Saturday morning, the distress calls started coming into the Coast Guard headquarters in Boston, which directs all operations from Rhode Island north to Canada. The first indication of the magnitude of the storm occurred when the radioman at Coast Guard Station Point Judith, Rhode Island, picked up a Mayday signal from a vessel thirty miles east of Block Island. The 76-foot wooden lobster boat *Determined*, with a crew of four, reported it was taking on water in heavy seas. Station Point Judith relayed the information to Lieutenant Robert Eccles at the command center in Boston. Eccles considered his options, and learned that the nearest large Coast Guard cutter was the 210-foot *Active*, only a few miles away from the Mayday location. The *Active*, commanded by Carl Helman, was returning from a month of patrolling the seas off Florida, and its crew was looking forward to their return to home port in Portsmouth, New Hampshire. Eccles diverted the ship from its northern path, and it swung around to the west, reaching the foundering fishing boat at 5:15 a.m.

"When we arrived at the vessel early Saturday morning," recalls Helman, "the wind was really blowing, and the seas were fifteen to twenty feet. We had established radio contact with the captain of the boat, and he thought maybe he and his crew could save the boat with one of our pumps. We could see that the *Determined* was taking a real beating from the seas, and we maneuvered as close as possible so that they would be on our lee side, and the *Active* would provide them a bit of protection from the wind."

The high seas also made it too dangerous for Helman to send the pump over in the cutter's 26-foot motor surfboat. Instead he ordered his men to use a firing gun to launch a line to the fishing vessel, which could then be used to haul the pump on board. When the line was fired it reached the *Determined* but became entangled in one of its outriggers, beyond the reach of the crew. (Outriggers are long poles extending from both sides of a vessel, designed to provide additional stability. At the end of the poles are "birds," or "divers," which can be lowered by chains into the sea. The missile-shaped birds are made from heavy steel, and when they are lowered approximately twenty feet below the sea's surface, their wings cause them to dive, pulling downward, which stabilizes the boat and minimizes rolling in heavy seas.)

Dave Nicholson, operations officer on the *Active*, describes what happened next: "It became a really tense situation at that point, because one of the *Determined* crewmen climbed out on the outrigger to free the line. We figured there was a good chance he might end up in the water, which would have been extremely dangerous in those seas."

Suspended above the angry seas and at the mercy of the wind, the crewman somehow kept his grip with one hand while he freed the line with the other. He then crawled back to the imperiled vessel, and his crew put the line through the winch and began hauling the line from the cutter to their boat. At the end of the line, in a waterproof container, came the pump, which they lifted on board and immediately put to work. The powerful pump kept up with the incoming seas, and eventually, after a couple of hours, it had sucked most of the water out of the bilge, while the *Active* stood by. The *Determined*'s captain felt the danger was over, and he radioed Nicholson, saying, "We're doing fine, and we all want to thank you for all your help."

Nicholson and Helman consulted their charts, ready to resume their planned trip north to New Hampshire. They noted that if they immediately headed for the Cape Cod Canal they would encounter adverse tides, so instead they decided to escort the *Determined* to Point Judith, and then steam through the canal when the tide changed. This decision probably saved the lives of the men on board the *Determined*.

An hour later, Nicholson happened to look across the tumultuous seas at the *Determined,* and he couldn't believe his eyes. "A crewman ran across the vessel in a Gumby suit [survival suit]," says Nicholson, "and he was waving his arms at us." A second later the captain's voice shouted over the radio, "Mayday, Mayday, Mayday! The boards are loose, we're going down!"

A wooden plank on the hull of the *Determined* had popped loose and water rushed in, flooding the bilge pumps. The man in the survival suit was joined by another and they leapt off the stern of the boat into the churning seas. A few seconds later the captain and the last crewmember, also in survival suits, followed the first two men and leapt off the ship.

Survival suits, also called immersion suits, are made from insulating material designed to delay the onset of hypothermia. The suits, including the hood, feet, and mitten-shaped hand coverings, are one piece with a zipper in the front that, once closed, seals the suit so that no water can leak inside. The survival suits not only protected the *Determined*'s crew from the cold temperature of the seas, but the orange color made the men more visible.

Nicholson sounded the man-overboard alarm, and the crew of the *Active* raced to their stations. Captain Helman supervised as Nicholson brought the *Active* as close as he dared to the two fishermen who had jumped first, while the crew lowered a scramble net over the side. The fishermen were up the net and safe aboard the cutter within a minute or two. Nicholson then maneuvered the *Active* to the other side of the *Determined,* where the last two crewmembers struggled to keep their heads above water. They were floating on the downwind side of their vessel and they were at risk of being slammed by its hull. Carefully, the *Active* was positioned between the men in the water and the *Determined,* to prevent the still spinning propellers of the lobster boat from killing the men. The men in the water grabbed hold of the scramble net, but only one of them had the strength to climb it. The remaining man in the water was too weak to do any more than grip the net. A Coast Guard swimmer, in full survival gear, descended the net and helped the last crewmember climb aboard the cutter.

Meanwhile, the *Determined,* now a ghost ship, continued to steam on, listing badly but managing to stay afloat even as waves washed completely over her. It wasn't until two hours later, at approximately 10 a.m., that Nicholson and the others watched her stern begin to settle beneath the sea's surface. Her bow pointed toward the gray sky and then it too slipped under the waves and the lobster boat commenced its fall to the bottom of the ocean.

When the *Active* was within a mile of Point Judith, a 41-foot utility boat was launched from the station, and the four fishermen, unnerved but not injured, were transferred aboard and brought ashore. Nicholson and Helman, relieved that the rescue was a success, turned their attention back to their original mission of heading home to New Hampshire.

The *Determined*'s bleak fate awaited other boats caught in the storm, making that Saturday one of the busiest and most stressful days in the history of the Coast Guard's service in the Northeast. In addition to cutters and patrol boats, Coast Guard aircraft also braved the storm, such as the helicopters that responded to a Mayday from a 59-foot stern trawler, the *Barbara and Christine,* out of New Bedford, Massachusetts. Laden with four thousand pounds of freshly caught fish, the trawler was taking on water at an alarming rate approximately eighteen miles southeast of Nantucket. The two helicopters fought their way through the swirling winds and airlifted the crew off the boat just minutes before it succumbed to the seas.

Although the *Determined* and the *Barbara and Christine* were lost, their crews were lucky because Coast Guard cutters and helicopters were just a short distance away. Out on Georges Bank, crews faced a different situation: there were no cutters in the area, and the storm was twice as powerful as it was just a hundred miles to the west, making rescue by helicopter impossible. For the crews of the vessels trapped on Georges Bank, survival would depend on their own courage and ingenuity and the assistance of fellow fishermen. One such vessel was the 70-foot dragger *Christina,* which had been fishing the northern end of Georges Bank. Her trouble started long before the storm reached its peak, when one of the vessel's outriggers broke, causing the boat to pitch wildly in the building seas. The *Christina*'s captain put out a Mayday call when it became clear that the boat might capsize if the storm continued to worsen.

Fifty miles away, Captain Jim Kendall, on board the 100-foot scalloper *Nordic Pride,* heard the Mayday. Kendall figured there might be another boat closer to the *Christina,* and he waited a minute, listening to the radio. When no one responded to the Mayday, Kendall picked up the radio microphone and told the *Christina*'s captain that he was on his way. He then called the Coast Guard and alerted them.

Before Kendall could reach the *Christina,* the stricken dragger's captain reported that things had taken a turn for the worse: the boat's mast had snapped at its base. Kendall advised him to cut the mast free of the boat, but the *Christina*'s captain refused, worried that they would lose radio communication. Kendall assured him that radio transmissions could reach him without the main antenna, but the men on the *Christina* were terrified of losing their only link to another boat, and did not take Kendall's prudent advice.

When Kendall was about a mile away the crew aboard the *Christina* suffered the consequences of their decision not to cut the mast. The base of the mast suddenly collapsed down through the deck and hit the generator, knocking it free of its cooling pipe. Seawater came gushing in through the broken pipe.

"We're abandoning ship!" said the *Christina*'s captain.

"Do you have survival suits?" asked Kendall.

"Negative! But we have to get in the life raft while there's time!"

"Can you hang on longer? We still haven't spotted you on radar!"

"We have to get off now! Hurry!"

The wind was now blowing at about 80 miles per hour, the air filled with scud, foam, and driving rain. Because the two boats were in a relatively shallow area of Georges Bank near Cultivator Shoal, the waves were steep and unpredictable. Kendall's radar picked up only clutter but somehow he found the sinking boat and the life raft just minutes after the crew had abandoned ship.

"Their life raft went so high up on the waves that it looked like they were on top of a mountain," says Kendall. "We were upwind, and I was worried the seas would push us on top of their raft, so we swung around and got downwind. My gang was on deck ready to try and haul them in, but the wind was so strong it pushed us away. I took a gamble and put the boat in reverse. Waves and spray were coming over the stern and I worried about losing one of my men. My guys threw a life ring to the raft, but the wind just whipped it back at us, hitting one of my crew in the head. The guys in the raft had a heaving donut attached to a thin line and they were able to throw that to us, and we pulled them to our boat. We had some of our gear called a chain bag over the side of the boat, which is mesh steel and can provide a hand- and foothold.

One of the men from the raft started up the chain bag, but then another one in the raft panicked and started climbing right up over his back. We were eventually able to get them all in."

When the rescued men were safely aboard the *Nordic Pride* they immediately kissed the deck. Kendall and his men took care of them, giving them cigarettes, clothes, and food. "We knew it could have just as easily been us," Kendall recalled. "It was an unbelievable feeling to get those men safely on board, but I couldn't really celebrate, we still had to steam out of that storm and go over a hundred miles just to get within a few miles of Nantucket. Later I was able to hand the wheel off to one of my men and I went down to talk to the guys we saved. I broke out some blackberry brandy and they all had a couple swigs. Then I noticed they were one guy short, and I said, 'Where's the kid?' This was the young crewmember that panicked and climbed over the back of his mate to get on board our ship. We went looking for him and found him in the cook's bunk with all the blankets up over his head. I told him I wanted to talk with him, but he wouldn't come out. I then ordered him out and made him take a sip of the brandy. He took a sip but then went right back under the blankets and never moved the whole trip back to port. I later learned he was never the same, and he committed suicide a few years later."

What Kendall and his crew would call the Thanksgiving Storm had now claimed three fishing boats but, like a hungry predator on the prowl, it still wanted more.

CHAPTER 6

Pitch-poled

THE CREW OF THE *FAIR WIND* LOOKED OUT AT SEAS that only a handful of people on earth have ever seen. It was now 11 a.m., and the waves had climbed to an unimaginable sixty to seventy feet of cresting fury. The boat's location, right on the edge of the continental shelf, was the very worst place to be. As the waves came off the deep water of the Atlantic and hit shallower waters on the shelf, they grew steeper, and the steeper the wave, the more likely it is to break upon itself and whatever else lies in its path. The waves had grown enormous; they literally could not support themselves, and the tops broke free of the main body of the wave and plunged straight downward, like an avalanche falling off a cliff. The wind, spiking at 90 miles per hour, added its blows to the giant combers by tearing off what was left of the wave top and flinging it through the air horizontally.

Despite the terrific beating, the men of the *Fair Wind* had faith in their boat. There was no sense of panic, just a sense of awe at the power of the storm and an impatience for it to move on. The sturdy little boat continued to meet every monstrous wave, and with a little help from Ernie on the throttle, she climbed up, up, up, ever higher until her bow was out of the water at the top of the wave. There was a split-second pause as the vessel hung on the crest of each wave with her propellers out of the water, spinning wildly and uselessly in the air and foam. Then, with the bow pointed downward, Ernie backed off the throttle and down she went, hitting the trough in a spray of water that shot upward like a geyser. Then, clenching the wheel, Ernie saw the next wave coming and gave the engine more diesel, as he positioned the bow yet again to take the wave head-on, and a couple degrees to port. Ernie may not have noticed it, but over the last couple of hours the interval between each wave had gotten shorter, allowing less and less time to recover from each punch. The crew felt like boxers in a ring, the ocean a quick, relentless opponent. They assumed they were suffering the storm's strongest punches, but in reality these waves were only jabs. The storm was still holding back.

Much of the time all Ernie could see out the windshield was foam and spray, but he had a sense of the spacing and timing between the waves, and he did his best to get ready for the next one. The vessel was doing almost everything Ernie asked of her, and with Garnos's instructions, the crew felt they could weather this monster. No serious thought was given to donning survival suits because the men, while concerned and exhausted, didn't feel any impending doom. Nor did they want to be encumbered by the suits, which made movement slow, and because of their mitten-like hand coverings the suits would make it difficult to pilot the boat or perform other tasks that had to be done in a split second.

Billy called the *Sea Fever* again, and this time the radio static made it difficult to hear Peter Brown. But at least he knew the vessel was still afloat when Peter's garbled voice responded. Billy also heard from another fishing boat, the *Broadbill*. He didn't wish this storm on even his worst enemy, but it was comforting to know he wasn't facing it alone. While it would be extremely difficult to maneuver to a boat in distress, Billy knew that all three boats would give it a try if necessary.

Billy had been through the stress of combat in Vietnam, and what was now happening on Georges Bank had a similar feel. His senses were in overdrive, and he felt wary, particularly because his enemy—the unrelenting waves—was impossible to predict. Sometimes they hit the boat from a slightly different angle, sometimes the waves came packed tightly together, and sometimes they varied in size. For six hours, Billy had been watching the huge dark walls of water advance toward the *Fair Wind,* and just when he thought they were due for a lull, more enormous waves rose out of the gloom. He wasn't saying much to the crew simply because there was nothing to say and nothing more they could do. They just had to stay sharp, be ready to react, and ride it out.

Ernie had been manning the wheel since 8 a.m., and Billy decided to take the next shift around 11:30 as the wind, unbelievably, was not abating, but still increasing in speed, now hitting an incredible 100 miles per hour. Billy took the wheel while in a trough, and Ernie stood beside him to port. On the opposite side of Billy, Rob Thayer stood ready to do whatever the skipper asked of him. Dave Berry was still in his bunk below.

Peering out the windshield, Ernie's face went pale and his eyes widened as the tallest wave yet, a wall of water close to one hundred feet tall, roared toward the *Fair Wind.* Billy held steady on the wheel and pushed more throttle, and the boat started to climb the vertical slope. None of the three men said a word, but all three must have been thinking the same thing, hoping to coax the *Fair Wind* forward. *Come on, come on, climb!*

As the vessel reached the halfway point up the wave, it seemed the propellers stopped biting because of all the foam, and Billy strained forward, willing his boat to climb still higher. For a half second, the boat hung on the face of the wave. Then the men, wide-eyed with terror, watched the curling summit of the wave top collapse on them. There was no time to shout, only a split second to brace themselves as tons of churning water crashed directly onto the *Fair Wind*. The impact, sounding like an explosion, spun the vessel 180 degrees, as if it were a toy. Anything not bolted down went flying, and the three men in the pilothouse struggled to remain standing and to avoid getting slammed into the walls or windshields. Dave Berry, still below, was likely hurled out of his bunk and into the air before crashing into the bunks opposite his.

In those agonizing slow-motion seconds, Ernie felt a sickening sensation as the *Fair Wind* careened wildly down the very wave it had tried to climb. The boat was in free fall, accelerating from the force of the wave on its stern until its nose smacked into the trough below, striking the ocean with incredible force. The bow bored into the sea, and Ernie felt the stern of the vessel, propelled by the avalanching wave behind the boat, go whipping up and over the submerged bow. Ernie smashed into the pilothouse ceiling, which was now below him. The *Fair Wind* had "pitch-poled," or flipped, and was now upside down.

Thousands of gallons of frigid water poured into the wheelhouse, seizing the men in a swirling embrace. In only a second or two, the now upside-down wheelhouse had almost completely filled with green seawater. Stunned, Ernie was tossed about as if in a washing machine. It was wet, cold, and dark, but he instinctively pushed upward and hit his head on the wheelhouse deck floor, where four or five inches of air had become trapped. Although he was totally disoriented, uncertain if he was upside down or right side up, his brain still screamed, *Get out, get out!* He took what air he could and ducked his head down into the water to try to figure out where he was. Below, he saw a faint patch of light. Deciding to swim for it, Ernie dove but hit his head on what may have been the windshield and he turned to go back for more air. But the air pocket had vanished. He thought to himself, It's all over. So this is how it happens. I'll be dead in a couple of minutes. Amazingly, he did not panic, nor shrink from confronting his death. He simply thought, If it's going to happen, it happens.

The survival instinct, however, is strong, and Ernie was not about to help the ocean do its dirty work. He still had one option left—besides giving up—and that was to go back down and swim toward the light.

Operating on adrenaline, he dove yet again, hoping the faint patch of light was an opening and not just a windshield. With lungs screaming for air, he slipped through a small hole. As soon as he felt his legs free of the boat, he looked in the direction he thought was the surface and stroked and kicked with all his strength. He couldn't hold his breath much longer, and he clawed his way through the water, knowing that if he didn't surface in a second or two, he would lose consciousness. The upward climb seemed an eternity, but just before he felt he would either breathe in the ocean or black out, his head cleared the surface. As he gasped for air, a wave washed over him, and he kicked furiously to raise his head a bit higher. Even when his head was above the wave, breathing was difficult because of the foam in the air. He was taking both air and water into his lungs.

Ernie saw the hull of the *Fair Wind,* and for a second this sight seemed so surreal, so strange, that his mind could not grasp what had happened. Amazingly, the boat's propeller still whirled at full speed, but Ernie couldn't hear the whine of the propeller over the howling wind and crashing seas. He had emerged on the windward side of the vessel and he tried to grip the overturned hull but found it impossible to secure a handhold on the smooth, slick metal. Although he tried to stay with it, the wind drove the boat away faster than he could swim, and he experienced a sense of deep dread; his only hope for survival was drifting away along with the boat.

All manner of debris, from lines to smashed pieces of wood, was swirling around as Ernie fought to stay with the boat, but with each passing second the *Fair Wind* was pushed farther away. Just staying afloat became a struggle for Ernie with his boots and jacket weighing him down. Fortunately, his boots were untied and he kicked them free, and then he squirmed out of his jacket. Exhausted, and barely able to move his arms, he spotted a bucket floating nearby and grabbed it, turned it over to trap some air inside, and used it as a float. The full magnitude of what had happened now hit him like a blow to the stomach. The situation looked hopeless, and already the cold November seas of 55 degrees were sucking the warmth out of his body and sapping what little strength he had left.

In a strange way, however, in those first few moments after capsizing, Ernie had already been lucky several times. First, he had stayed conscious, despite being thrown about in the pilothouse. Second, the fact that he did not have a survival suit on saved his life: its buoyancy would have prevented him from swimming downward toward the opening in the pilothouse. And, when he did surface, it was away from the slicing propeller. He also had the good fortune to have his boots untied or he would have surely sank under their weight. And finally, the bucket floated within reach as if guided there by the very wind and waves that had pitch-poled the *Fair Wind*.

Yes, a few small strokes of luck fell Ernie's way, but now, with the boat drifting away and Ernie fighting to stay afloat in the unrelenting seas, he was going to need more than luck to survive; he'd need a miracle.

CHAPTER 7

Decisions

S O FAR, IN A HUNGRY SEA THAT AFFORDED NO SEC-
ond chances, Ernie had made all the right decisions. But
now he had an agonizing choice: to continue clinging to
the plastic bucket for buoyancy or risk letting it go and trying to
somehow claw his way back to the *Fair Wind*. If he did not make
it to the boat, he knew he would be lost in the abyss of unfor-
giving seas. He'd be dead within an hour.

Panting with exhaustion, and dressed only in socks, jeans, and
a sweatshirt, Ernie tightly hugged the bucket, his only ally against
the storm. In many ways, Ernie's predicament mirrored that of
the fishermen who had plied these waters more than a century
earlier. Those men left their schooners in small dories to haul in
their catch, and if the weather turned against them they couldn't
always make it back to the mother ship. Many died after the wind
and waves separated them from their schooners, and then snow,
rain, darkness, or fog closed in like a curtain, eliminating visibility and any hope of finding the ship.

Ernie tried to gather his wits and consider his next move, but it was difficult to think clearly in that violent world of waves and wind. When the sea wasn't crashing on top of him, the salty spray came hurtling across its surface, stinging his face and eyes and smacking his head like buckshot. The mental strain was tremendous; in the span of a few minutes he had gone from riding out the storm in the pilothouse to facing what he thought was certain death when the *Fair Wind* pitch-poled. And now he was fighting to stay afloat in the open ocean. Overwhelmed, Ernie needed time to collect his thoughts, but the sea, cold and impersonal, refused to let him rest. The *Fair Wind* was more than fifty feet away and quickly drifting further.

Intuitively, Ernie knew that the temporary comfort of the bucket was just that, temporary, and that his only hope for survival was to get back to the boat and stay with it. For some of us, this might have been the moment when we hung our heads and gave up, or denied the reality of the situation and stayed with the bucket. Somehow, however, Ernie resisted the temptation to do either. Reluctantly and with a sense of trepidation, he let the bucket go and faced the void alone. With what little strength he had left he started swimming toward the *Fair Wind*. The same waves that pushed the boat away were now helping Ernie along, and he found that if he timed his kicking just right, he could actually bodysurf down the face of a wave by stretching his arms out directly in front of him. When each house-sized wave broke on him, he struggled back to the surface and then swam again until he felt the next wave propel him forward, bodysurfing as best he could toward the overturned hull. The hull came in and out of view, disappearing when Ernie was in a trough but reappearing whenever he was lifted by a wave.

After riding five or six waves he reached the *Fair Wind,* but as before, he found it impossible to climb on top of the slimy hull. Surrounded by foam and shrieking wind, Ernie found it difficult to tell if the propeller was still turning. He decided to avoid the stern and the potentially deadly slicing of the propeller and instead turned toward the bow. As he kicked and stroked, he could feel his power diminish with each move and realized he had only a few more minutes of strength left before he would no longer be able to keep his head above the foam. Each time a wave buried him, he fought to the surface for a quick breath of precious oxygen before the next one came. His heart pounded so hard it felt like it might explode.

Because he was in the water and not on the hull, he was losing body heat approximately twenty-four times faster than he would in air of the same temperature. He had been immersed in the ocean for half an hour, and his dexterity was starting to suffer along with his energy. The immense size of the waves did not help his chances; the higher the waves, the more energy a survivor spends just trying to keep his head above water, and the expended effort only adds to the speed of the chilling hypothermia moving inward from the body's extremities. It is known that waves over twenty feet hurt survival chances significantly, and Ernie was locked in hand-to-hand combat with waves three times that size. If he did not get out of the water soon, all of his luck and good decisions would be wasted, serving only to postpone the inevitable.

As he rounded the bow, he saw an incredible sight on the other side of the hull: a rubber life raft, fully inflated. It was a bright orange, round, dome-canopied raft, approximately six feet in diameter, tethered by a long line to the *Fair Wind*. Ernie's heart soared. Not only did he see an opportunity to escape the bone-chilling water, but hope returned that the other crewmen had gotten out of the boat and were inside the raft. He swam toward the raft, careful to keep out of the way of the drifting *Fair Wind*, which threatened to overtake him.

The six-man Givens life raft looked like a small tent resting atop two large donut-shaped tubes. A fabric floor stretched across its bottom, and inflatable ribs led to the top, where a tiny beacon was mounted. For stability, a large ballast bag hung on the bottom underwater. It was designed to flood with 2,900 pounds of water, and this weight would hold the raft upright in heavy seas and prevent it from flipping over and tumbling across the ocean's surface.

The raft had been mounted atop the pilothouse in a container designed, should the vessel capsize, to float free of the boat and then self-inflate from CO_2 cartridges inside. Fortunately, the tether from the raft down to the boat had been long enough for the raft to reach the surface. Had that tether been just five feet shorter, the raft would not have reached the surface and instead would have been torn from the line by the seas and blown away.

When Ernie reached the raft, he managed to use the small boarding ladder to heave himself up and crawl inside. No one was inside. He collapsed on the floor of the raft and held back a cry of anguish.

Although Ernie was finally out of the sea, the waves still pummeled him, crashing atop the raft and crushing him into the fabric floor. Yet he was spared their full force because the raft was floating on the lee side of the hull, which partially protected him from the towering walls of water. Four or five inches of water sloshed around the bottom, so he tried to find a sitting position with his back against the dome to keep some of his body out of the water. The raft itself was being jerked violently on its tether and Ernie feared the line might tear the raft's fabric at the point where it was secured. But he would not set the raft free. My friends are down there, he thought. He still held out hope that maybe, just maybe, one of them would emerge from the boat, and he'd be able to haul him in. Perhaps, he thought, they were already free of the boat and he simply couldn't see them in the churning water and foam. Billy Garnos, Rob Thayer, and Dave Berry; one or all of them might make it, he told himself. But deep inside he knew the odds were incredibly low. Still, he held his silent vigil alongside the overturned *Fair Wind* and refused to release the raft from its line.

Icy water poured into the raft, and the curtained doorway did little to stop the flood. The tether was tied to the raft directly in front of the raft's entrance hole, which meant the opening faced into the wind and oncoming seas. The walls of the raft did little to muffle the roaring and hissing of the waves. Every now and then Ernie stuck his head out of the raft's opening to look for another survivor, but all he could see was the ocean washing over the *Fair Wind*'s hull. There was no horizon, no sky, just moving hills of gray and green. He was shivering now, and his soggy sweatshirt seemed to make him feel colder, but he knew any material around his skin was better than none. His sweatshirt, jeans, and socks added a slight degree of warmth because they trapped a bit of water warmed by his body. He looked up and saw a small bag hanging on the wall of the canopy and reached up and snagged it. Inside was a small plastic tag of instructions about the raft. With the raft pitching wildly it was difficult to read, but Ernie managed to decipher the first of several instructions, which said to free the raft from the tether as soon as possible. A minute later a wave slammed into the raft and, as he fell forward, the instruction tag came loose and went out with the cascading water.

Ernie brought himself back to a sitting position and poked his head out of the raft, looking at the bowline knot that secured the line to the raft, now knowing he should release the knot immediately. He had been inside the raft for thirty minutes. He looked at the *Fair Wind*'s hull and decided that until it settled farther down in the water he would not release the raft. He simply could not leave as long as even a shred of hope remained that his friends were alive. What he didn't know was that the constant tugging of the raft on the line was doing damage to the ballast bag beneath him.

CHAPTER 8

The *Sea Fever*

PPROXIMATELY TEN MILES NORTH OF WHERE ERNIE was struggling to stay alive, the ferocious storm was battering another boat, the *Sea Fever*. The *Sea Fever* was similar in size and shape to the *Fair Wind*, but this 50-foot lobster boat was made of wood rather than steel. Both its hull and superstructure were painted white, and the front of the pilothouse had four windows made of heavy safety glass, each approximately eighteen inches wide and twelve inches tall. There was a window and a plywood wall on the port side, and a window and a two-panel door made of three-quarter-inch plywood on the starboard side. Clear plastic weather strips hung from the rear of the pilothouse, allowing quick access to the work deck. Below were the engine compartment, galley, and four bunks outfitted with seatbelts so that sleeping crewmen would not be tossed out of bed if the seas kicked up.

The *Sea Fever* was owned by Bob Brown, who later purchased the *Andrea Gail*, whose demise was chronicled in Sebastian Junger's *The Perfect Storm*. Brown had the *Sea Fever* built exactly to his specifications in 1970, and it was his first offshore boat. A few years later, he purchased a second lobster boat, the 70-foot *Sea Star.* On Saturday, November 22, 1980, both boats were ambushed on Georges Bank by the sudden storm that capsized the *Fair Wind.* Bob was captaining the *Sea Star;* his twenty-two-year-old son, Peter, was captaining the *Sea Fever.*

Peter, who was six feet tall with blue eyes, brown hair, and an easy smile, had a demeanor almost opposite that of his unyielding father. While his hard-driving father pushed his crew to the limit of their endurance and even jeopardized their safety, Peter understood that a crew could get just as much accomplished in a more relaxed atmosphere where each individual felt he was part of a team. Peter even encouraged suggestions from the crew, whereas Bob typically glared at the crewman who offered a suggestion, then told him to get back to work. Consequently, the men who worked for both the Browns wrangled for future trips with Peter rather than Bob, and Peter was more than happy to captain the *Sea Fever* to get out from under the critical eye of his father.

On the Saturday of the storm, Peter's crew included three young men, all of whom had been working on the *Sea Fever* since the start of the season. Gary Brown (no relation to Bob or Peter) was the oldest of the group at age twenty-five and was the only married crewmember. His wife, Honour, was pregnant with their first child, and Gary, who loved to fish even for recreation, was already talking about how someday he would own his own boat and teach his son or daughter all about commercial fishing. From the moment Honour first met Gary, she knew fishing was his life, and she accepted that. Living in Plymouth, Massachusetts, afforded Gary plenty of opportunities to fish, and friends were amazed that even after working on the *Sea Fever* for five straight days, he'd spend his day off back on the water surf-casting for stripers, or paddling a canoe on a pond in search of trout.

Gary and Honour had a strong marriage, and they often celebrated his return from Georges Bank by going out with friends for Chinese food and then taking in a movie. Sometimes Gary would surprise his wife by bringing home lobster, scallops, or swordfish and preparing a great meal for just the two of them. Gary did this in spite of Bob Brown's policy of not allowing any of the crew to take home the catch. The year before he worked for Peter, he was working on the *Sea Star* for Bob, and Gary decided to smuggle two large lobsters off the boat. As the boat was nearing its home port, Gary secretly took the lobsters out of the tank and put them in his duffel bag. As the crew prepared to leave the boat under Bob Brown's watchful eye, Gary's duffel bag, which lay on the deck, started to move. Fellow crewman Richard Rowell whispered and motioned to Gary that his bag was "walking" and Gary quickly picked up the bag, slung it over his shoulder, and walked by Bob Brown, wishing him a nice weekend. Bob was none the wiser and that night Gary and Honour enjoyed another of Gary's great seafood dinners.

Friends of Gary knew him as a handsome, feisty Irishman with red hair and freckles. He was five feet eleven inches tall with a barrel chest and built like a rock. Peter thought of Gary as the perfect crewmember because he'd never let anyone outwork him. He had a great sense of humor and almost always had a big smile on his face. Peter recognized that besides Gary's strong work ethic, he was reliable and quite handy, and he made him the deck boss of the *Sea Fever*.

The other two crewmembers, Richard Rowell and Brad Bowen, loved working on the *Sea Fever*, in large part because of their good-natured captain and deck boss. Rowell, at age twenty-one, was the older of the two and had been in the marines, rising to the rank of sergeant. When his hitch in the service was up he returned to his hometown of Danvers, Massachusetts, and looked for work. The first job he took was at a machine shop, but like Ernie Hazard he found working indoors stifling. His co-workers didn't appreciate how Rowell propped open the doors to the shop in the dead of winter to let in the fresh air. A friend suggested Rowell join him in commercial fishing, saying, "If you want to make money, get on one of Bob Brown's boats." But when Rowell tracked down Brown and asked for a job, Brown took a cold look at Rowell's five-foot-six-inch frame and said, "Forget it, you're too small to handle the work on my boats." Rowell didn't argue, didn't tell him about his service in the marines, but instead simply said, "Just give me a chance."

Bob Brown may have been difficult to work for, but he was fair. If someone asked for a chance, Bob was likely to grant one, and then watch him crumble after a few days of working around the clock at sea. Bob was tough as nails, and he expected his crewmembers to be the same, or they didn't last more than a trip or two.

Brown was also short in stature, and as he sized up Rowell, he might have seen something of himself in the young greenhorn. Sheer muscle and size weren't the only factors for work on a boat—stamina and endurance were equally important, and more than once Brown had outworked larger, stronger men, leaving them gasping like fish that had just been gaffed while he continued to haul gear as if he was just getting started.

"Be ready to go in a couple days," Brown said to Rowell.

On that first trip, Rowell had to endure the demands of Bob Brown, who treated new crew like slaves. This was likely Brown's way of quickly weeding out the slackers, and Rowell wasn't going to give Brown anything to complain about. He was a dynamo on deck, and although Brown never once gave him a compliment, Rowell knew he had cemented a position as a permanent crewman when Brown started calling him "Sarge" after he learned of Rowell's military experience. The nickname stuck.

As Sarge learned the business, he heard how other owners were far more flexible with their crews, but he also knew that when you fished on a boat owned by Bob Brown, you almost always made good money. The money Sarge made was not paid to him after each trip as it was on most other lobster boats; instead Brown would give the crew a small weekly check, and the majority of what each man made wasn't paid until the end of the year. Although other crewmen grumbled, Sarge didn't mind having most of his pay withheld because it was a good forced saving plan. He wasn't about to piss away his hard-earned paychecks, and this method ensured that didn't happen. It also guaranteed that he'd have plenty of money to pay his income taxes at the year's end since no taxes were withheld from his pay. Bob Brown kept meticulous records and was more than fair, and at the end of season he and Sarge would sit down and go over each trip Sarge had worked that year. Some people thought Brown followed this practice to keep the money working longer for himself, but the real reason had nothing to do with the time value of money and everything to do with ensuring he had a crew when cold weather hit. Brown did not believe in ending his trips to Georges Bank just because the snow was flying. When he first started offshore lobster fishing with only the *Sea Fever*, he'd work that boat straight through the year, including winter. Later, when he bought the larger *Sea Star*, he kept the *Sea Fever* in port during the winter, but continued his trips to Georges Bank in the larger *Sea Star* every month of the year. Invariably some of the crew, after having a successful spring, summer, and fall, wanted to call it quits when the freezing weather hit. Bob Brown had long since learned that when a crewmember left in the late fall it was tough to find a replacement. He solved that problem by explaining to his crew that when you signed on with him it was for the entire "season," and the season didn't end until January. Then, for the next year, the crew he signed up had to get through the winter months if they wanted to work the warmer season ahead. Bob Brown was no fair-weather fisherman, and that was one of the first things his crews learned.

During that first year, Sarge also worked on Bob Brown's other boat, the *Sea Fever*. Sarge found that Peter had much of his father's "sea smarts" but without the inflexible edge. While Bob Brown would haul gear in dangerous conditions, Peter knew when to stop for the safety of the crew. Peter once said to Sarge, "The fish will still be there when the seas ease up."

The fourth crewman aboard the *Sea Fever* during the November storm was Bradford Bowen. The nineteen-year-old had grown up in Connecticut, where he attended a private school and played hockey, developing into one of the state's top players. But the 6 a.m. practices and grueling schedule of games took their toll on Brad, and when it came time for college, he had had enough of hockey, and he passed on exploring athletic scholarships. Instead he decided to pursue his passion for skiing and attended the University of Utah. The relief from hockey and the enjoyment of skiing were so great that after just one semester of school Brad decided to take some time off so he could ski almost every day and work odd jobs at night. When spring rolled around he headed back to New England and started looking for work. He had a cousin who was an inshore lobster fisherman in Marblehead, Massachusetts, and Brad asked him about opportunities as a fisherman. Brad got the same advice Sarge received: "If you don't mind working your tail off, contact Bob Brown, because his boats make the most money." Brad met with Bob and within days he was at work mending gear, getting ready for the upcoming season. Brad's initial opinion of Bob Brown was similar to Sarge's. "Bob Brown was almost ruthless the way he drove us," recalled Brad, "and if I did something wrong he'd sure let me know about it. Giving compliments for good work was just not in his mindset—he expected everything to be done perfectly and quickly."

When the season started, however, Lady Luck shined on Brad

and he was assigned to the *Sea Fever,* captained by Peter Brown, with Gary Brown as the deck boss. "Gary was a great teacher," said Brad. "I learned about the boat, the sea, and lobsters all at once. Gary was like a big brother to me, and when I saw he had a tattoo of a lobster on his arm, one of the first things I did when we were back in port was to have the same tattoo put on my arm." He also learned from Peter and Sarge, and what really stuck in his mind was hearing Sarge say that working on the boat was tougher than the marines. "I loved a challenge, and I took that to heart. I had a sense of satisfaction that I was succeeding at something extremely difficult. And we were paid well for what we did, which is the ultimate incentive."

Brad's initiation in commercial fishing wasn't all smooth sailing, however. Twice the first season he fell overboard when he lost his footing from the momentum of dropping a trap over. Each time when he got back on board, shaken and unnerved, he shouted, "I quit!" But after a few hours he'd change his mind. The third time he went overboard he came within a minute of losing his life. He had just dropped a trap over and the line to the trap wrapped around his ankle, pulling him off the boat. Sarge saw what happened and shouted at Brad, "Are you in the lines?" Brad was on the surface and screamed yes. Sarge asked the question because he knew the weight of the trap made it impossible to haul the line back in by hand, so the crew scrambled to get their end of the line through the hauler. Meanwhile, Brad knew that within a second or two the slack in the line was going to be taken up by the sinking trap. He pulled his fourteen-inch Dexter knife from its sheath on his belt, took one big breath, and went down, bending over at the waist so he could reach the rope. On his first try his knife cut through the line, freeing him from a trip to the bottom of the sea.

The crew hauled him on board, and again Brad looked at Peter and stammered, "I quit." Once Peter determined Brad was

OK, he said, "You can't quit, you just tied the boat record for the number of times one crewman has gone overboard! If you stick around you'll have the record all to yourself!"

Brad didn't quit and he stayed on as the fourth crewmember of the *Sea Fever* for the 1980 season. He thought he'd seen the worst his newfound profession could throw at him. But the November storm would terrify him in an entirely new and agonizingly slow way.

CHAPTER 9

Blow-out

L IKE THE *FAIR WIND*, THE *SEA FEVER* ARRIVED ON Georges Bank early Saturday morning, and the crew hoped to begin working at daylight. Peter Brown awoke at 3 a.m and noticed the boat was riding more roughly than it had been at midnight but not enough to cause alarm and he went back to sleep. By 4:30 a.m., however, the motion of the boat was so violent he woke up with a start and immediately climbed the stairs to the pilothouse. Gary Brown was on the wheel. Gary looked at Peter, shook his head, and muttered, "So much for good weather." It was still dark, but judging from the pitching of the boat, Peter estimated that the waves were fifteen to twenty feet. Outside, the wind howled and the plastic weather strips in the back of the pilothouse snapped every which way. Rain fell in torrents, splattering the boat and adding to the din of the wind and waves.

"We obviously aren't going to be doing any fishing for a while," said Peter. "Why don't you get Brad and Sarge up, and I'll move us into fifty fathoms." He took the helm from Gary and turned the boat northwest and into the wind. Should the weather get worse,

Peter did not want to get caught where they were: between Munson and Powell Canyons at the southeastern edge of Georges Bank. The topography of the ocean floor in this section of Georges Bank is characterized by mountains and valleys and can drop from sixty to six hundred fathoms in just a quarter mile. That variation, coupled with the warm eddies from the Gulf Stream, can produce some of the worst upwelling and turbulence of water anywhere, steepening waves and causing them to crest and break.

Peter steamed northwest to an area with a fairly uniform bottom, fifty to sixty fathoms deep, then just held position with the bow pointed into the seas. Soon the updated 5 a.m. forecast came over the radio, and he shook his head in disgust as he listened to a markedly different report from the last broadcast at 11 p.m. This report now included a gale warning and predicted that the seas would grow to between eight and fourteen feet. Not only is the forecast late and of no value, thought Peter, but it's underestimating the conditions we're already in. He picked up the radio microphone and called another lobster boat riding out the storm nearby: "*Sea Fever* calling *Broadbill*." Captain Grant Moore of the *Broadbill* answered, and each gave their positions. "We're just jogging along," said Peter, "and got her headed into the seas, holding position. What's going on with this weather? This is no gale, it's a storm; we've got winds gusting up to sixty [knots]." Moore, whose vessel was about fifteen miles west of the *Sea Fever*, had no more answers than Peter did but said he'd check back with him in an hour.

Spray from the waves washed over the pilothouse and down onto the *Sea Fever*'s deck, and several inches of water sloshed around Peter's feet beneath the wheel. The whole crew was now gathered in the pilothouse, and although Sarge and Brad were still pretty green, they knew enough to be concerned. "All I had to do was look at Peter's face and I could see he was worried," recalled Brad. "I knew he was thinking ahead, trying to make sure we'd be in the best shape we could possibly be in if things got worse. This was the first storm I'd ever been in, so I just waited for instructions. I watched Peter goose the engine to get us up and over the waves and then ease off as we went down their backside. It seemed each hour the waves grew larger and by midmorning there were some that were forty to fifty feet. No one had to tell me this was trouble, I could see it in their eyes. We all put life jackets on. We probably would have put survival suits on if we could have maneuvered in them. That's how bad it was getting."

The seas had grown so violent that the fifty-pound bait boxes lashed to the deck came loose and began sliding back and forth in the deck water, sometimes blocking the scuppers that allowed water to drain from the enclosed deck. The water pouring onto the deck was rising, so Gary and Brad went to fix the problem. On the deck, Brad had to crawl to escape the force of the wind. "I just could not believe the wind—if I stuck my head up past the gunnels it felt like getting slapped. I couldn't hear anything other than the wind roaring in my ears, and there was foam scudding through the air mixed with the rain. I was worried a big wave was going to sweep over the boat and take me with it. Gary and I worked as fast as we could. We grabbed those bait boxes and just hurled them overboard."

At 11 a.m. the men heard the updated weather forecast for Georges Bank, which was finally catching up with reality. Still, however, the report was understated: "Storm warning, wind northwest forty to fifty knots, diminishing overnight to west at twenty to twenty-five knots Sunday. Rain and fog ending late Saturday afternoon. Seas fifteen to twenty-five feet Saturday, subsiding Saturday night." This was the first report that mentioned a storm, but the storm had been raging for six hours. The wind and wave predictions would have to be doubled to match what was happening just beyond the windows of the *Sea Fever*.

The advancing waves were the size of two- and three-story

homes, and the length of the troughs between each oncoming wave varied. Sarge had never witnessed conditions even remotely like this, and mixed with his apprehension was a feeling of pure awe. The power of both wind and sea was almost beyond human comprehension. His senses were electric. He felt ready to spring into action, but he wasn't sure what that action would be. In the meantime, he braced himself as best he could as the deck heaved and pitched, and he kept a wary eye on each advancing wave.

On the radio, Peter raised his father, Bob Brown, who was twenty miles to the east on the 70-foot steel-hulled *Sea Star.* Through the static Sarge heard Bob Brown say that he too was taking a pounding, and there was nothing that could be done but ride it out. When Bob added that he'd never seen anything like this, Sarge felt an involuntary shudder go through him. When Bob Brown says this is unbelievable, thought Sarge, we're in trouble.

As the boat climbed the next wave, Sarge couldn't decide which was worse: the moment when the boat reached the top of the wave and both the bow and stern were momentarily out of the water or when the boat slid down to the bottom of the trough between waves and the bow hit with a bang. Each time she struck the trough, Sarge steadied himself as spray flew and the boat shook. Sea and foam enveloped the bow, and Sarge held his breath waiting for the *Sea Fever* to reassert herself. As the boat came back up, the process repeated itself as the vessel climbed the next big comber heading toward them.

The sturdy *Sea Fever* withstood each and every wave until approximately 12:30 p.m. That's when it happened. Peter looked up to see an enormous wave rearing out of the tempest, making the hairs on the back of his neck stand on end. The wave seemed to be nearly twice the size of the others, and on its top was a fifteen-foot breaking comber. He gave the boat more throttle and then watched in horror as the wave hurled its full fury down on the vessel.

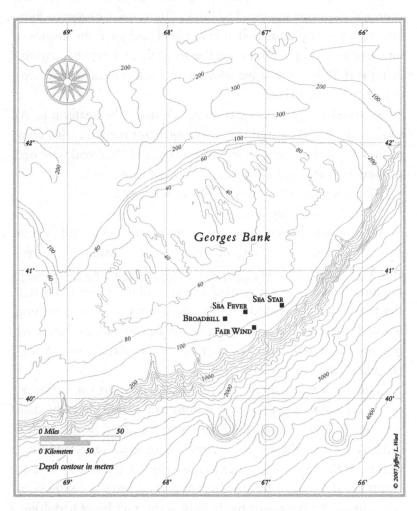

Approximate locations of the boats at 11:30 a.m. on Saturday, November 22, 1980, as wind speeds at Georges Bank reached a terrifying 100 miles per hour and waves topped fifty feet.

He then heard an ear-splitting *pow!*

The water, as if concrete, hit the windshield, blasting away two of the four panels of the pilothouse. Torrents flooded in. As the wave struck, Peter managed to duck. The impact staggered him, but somehow he remained at the wheel and gave the engine a bit more juice, hoping to power the vessel up and over the smothering surf before the wave spun them back down, as had happened to the *Fair Wind*.

Without the windows, the ocean's roar was deafening. As soon as the vessel cleared the wave top, Peter turned to his crew to find out if they were alive. Sarge, Gary, and Brad had returned to their feet, stunned, shaken, and wet but uninjured.

"We gotta turn her around!" Peter screamed.

"Do it!" Gary shouted.

If there's one maneuver mariners dread most, it's turning a boat around in huge seas, and it's never done unless absolutely necessary. Yet the move was imperative. If Peter kept the *Sea Fever* heading into the seas, the waves would soon send more water through the two shattered window openings. No amount of pumping would be able to keep up with a continual onslaught of seawater pouring through the window openings, and eventually one of several bleak outcomes would result.

The rising water might kill the engine or short the batteries, or it could create such a great amount of shifting weight that, with the help of a wave, the boat could roll. And finally, even if the boat escaped those fates, it could become so heavy and sluggish from the incoming water that it simply wouldn't be able to climb the next wave. In this case she would broach—slide sideways down the wave—or pitch-pole as the *Fair Wind* had done.

There was no time for Peter to choose a particular trough for the turn and no time to talk it over with Gary, the most seasoned of the rest of the crew. He simply had to make the turn now, before the next wave hit. As the *Sea Fever* slid down the back of the enormous wave that had smashed the windows, Peter waited until he felt she was in the trough and then he punched the engine to almost full power and started a tight turn to port. Holding his breath, he took a quick glance out the starboard window. Through the rain he saw the next wave barreling toward the boat like a raging bull, as if it were trying to catch him beam-on, before the turn was complete. He had maybe eight seconds maximum to make the turn, or the wave would catch the *Sea Fever* in the exposed position, and finish her off.

CHAPTER 10

Swept Away

CCORDING TO COAST GUARD MARINE CASUALTY
reports, the loss of windshield panels due to breaking
seas is the genesis of countless serious accidents and
sinkings. Losing the windshield itself may not be the final failure
of the boat, but it is often the first thing that goes wrong, lead-
ing to a host of complications that even the best of captains cannot overcome. And the vulnerability of windshields, windows,
and portholes is not limited to small boats like the *Sea Fever*, but
extends to giant ships and drilling rigs as well. One of the worst
accidents in the North Atlantic in the last fifty years started with
a blown window on the *Ocean Ranger*, a mammoth oil drilling
rig stationed 166 nautical miles east of St. John's, Newfoundland.
Weighing fifteen thousand tons, the rig towered over the sea and
carried a crew of eighty-four. It contained recreation rooms, a
library, a mess hall, offices, machine shops, a communication
room, a navigation bridge, and several small power plants. In normal seas, the men who worked on board said it didn't even feel
like the oil rig was on the ocean because only the largest waves

could lift the rig's heavy bulk. The ballast control room was situated below the rig's lower deck, but it was still thirty-two feet above the ocean. The room was circular with four glass portholes, eighteen inches in diameter.

On February 14, 1981, the *Ocean Ranger's* crew was aware that the National Weather Service had issued a severe storm warning, but there was little concern on board. The oil rig had recently come through other storms without any trouble, and most felt the *Ranger* was a steel fortress able to withstand anything the seas threw its way. The engineers who designed it claimed the *Ranger* was unsinkable and that storm-induced waves would slip harmlessly between the rig's support columns. The storm barreling down on the *Ranger,* however, was similar in its ferocity to the one that ambushed the *Sea Fever* and the *Fair Wind,* with hurricane-force winds and enormous seas.

The first indication of trouble on the *Ocean Ranger* occurred at 8:44 p.m., when the rig's commander radioed St. John's that "a wave has taken a window out of the control room. Mopping up, no problems." Unfortunately, the crew's problems were just beginning. Seas had soared to a height of sixty feet, and the control room's wet electrical panel was shocking the operators. One operator even radioed that electronically controlled ballast valves were opening on their own. Yet the *Ranger's* commander told St. John's that they were doing fine and riding out the storm.

Almost four hours passed before the ocean got the upper hand. Suddenly, at 12:52 a.m., the *Ranger's* radio crackled to life, "*Mayday! Mayday!* We have a severe list and require immediate attention." This was followed by several more Mayday calls, explaining that the crew was preparing to take to lifeboats.

A supply ship, the *Seaforth Highlander,* was in the vicinity of the *Ranger,* and it fought the huge seas to reach the crippled rig. When the ship arrived, its crew watched in horror as one of the *Ranger* lifeboats capsized, spilling the men inside into the frigid seas. The

Highlander's crew threw lines and a life raft to the men floundering in the water, but hypothermia had drained their strength and one by one they were carried away by the mountainous waves. Other supply ships arrived at the scene, but like the men on the *Highlander,* they spotted only lifeless bodies being tossed about by the seas. At 3:15 a.m, the *Ranger* itself succumbed to the storm and toppled into the sea.

All eighty-four crewmen on the *Ocean Ranger* died that night. While the cause of death was listed as hypothermia and drowning, it was the blown porthole in the control room that doomed the men. When water entered through the shattered window it shorted out the control panel, and valves that should have been closed opened on their own, allowing seawater to flood ballast tanks and eventually overturn the *Ranger.*

Unlike the captain of the *Ocean Ranger,* Peter Brown knew instantly he was facing a critical problem when the windshield panels exploded. His decision to turn the *Sea Fever* and go with following seas rather than ride head on into the waves was the right reaction to the emergency. He needed to shelter the bow from the oncoming seas to stop the flow of incoming water as well as to attempt to patch the windows.

As Peter turned the boat, Gary, Sarge, and Brad clung to whatever they could in the pilothouse, knowing that they might get slammed by a wave before the maneuver was complete. They all now understood that they were caught in a life-or-death situation, which might be decided in the next few seconds. No one said a word, and each kept his fears to himself.

Finally, as the *Sea Fever* completed the turn, they collectively exhaled.

The crew's relief was short-lived, however, because a second later a wave caught the boat and hurled it forward. The *Sea Fever* didn't simply ride the giant comber but seemed to fly above it for a hundred feet. A thundering whooshing noise accompanied its flight through the foamy water. Peter let the breaker pass under the boat and then adjusted his speed to ride on the back of the wave and stay ahead of the next wave's crest. He worked the throttle carefully to keep the *Sea Fever* running at approximately the same speed as the wave. He opened the throttle for a second or two whenever he felt the bow drop and eased off when it lifted too high. Then he turned to Gary and shouted, "Take the wheel! We've got to get these windows patched so we can turn back into it!"

While Sarge and Brad scrambled to bring plywood, hammer, and nails from below, Gary took the wheel, and Peter reached out to the deck and pulled in a coil of nylon rope. The rope was to be his lifeline; Peter had decided that he would be the one to go out on the bow and fix the windows—he felt it was his duty as captain to be the one to take the risk. Sarge would grip the other end of the line, and should Peter go over, they figured they would stand at least a fifty-fifty chance of hauling him back on board.

When the line was secure around Peter's waist, he leaned toward Brad, and just inches from his ear shouted, "When I'm out on the bow, pass the hammer and nails through the broken window and then do the same with the plywood."

Brad never had a chance to answer. A wave of approximately seventy feet bore down on the men with a furious rush, breaking just off her stern. The force and the speed of the snarling curler sent the crippled boat careening down its face faster than the screws could turn.

"I can't control it!" screamed Gary.

He could feel that the propeller had stopped biting, and steering was nonexistent, and in a sickening sideways movement, the *Sea Fever* broached. The boat was caught sideways, or "beam-to," in the driving onslaught of the sea.

A second later the wave lifted the port side up and drove the starboard side downward. The force knocked the men from their feet and threw them into the air as they heard a terrific *crack!*

The water's impact was so violent that it blew apart most of the starboard side of the pilothouse as if it had been hit by a giant fist. In came the rushing water with a great roar, engulfing all four of the crew. Then, as the boat righted itself, the water rushed out of the pilothouse, sucking Gary and Sarge up from the floor and toward the splintered opening.

The pilothouse was in shambles, littered with shards of wood and glass, and adding to the confusion was the continual blasting buzz of the bilge alarm, signaling that the bottom of the boat had rapidly filled with water. Peter and Brad struggled to their feet and looked through the busted opening. They witnessed a miracle and a nightmare. Sarge was lying up against the rail, the only thing separating him from the ocean, but Gary was out of the boat, floating faceup in the seas with a stunned look on his face.

While Peter took the wheel, Brad helped Sarge up and he and Sarge ran out on the deck. They threw a life ring to Gary, but the wind just whipped it back. A wave crashed over him and he was lost from sight.

"I've lost him!" screamed Brad. "I can't see him!"

"There he is!" shouted Sarge, pointing directly behind the boat. Now the boat was floating thirty feet from Gary. "Don't take your eyes off him!" he shouted to Brad.

Sarge grabbed a line to throw to Gary, but by the time he was ready, Gary had drifted almost fifty feet from the *Sea Fever.* There was no way the line would reach him in the wind. "Hang on, Gary!" he screamed.

Realizing the futility of trying to reach Gary with a rope, Brad started to climb up the rail to dive in.

"No!" shouted Sarge as he grabbed Brad's coat and yanked him back on deck. "Listen to me! Stay in the fucking boat!" Sarge knew that it was going to be difficult to get one man back, and impossible to get two.

Meanwhile, Peter had run down the stairs and into the engine room. Two feet of water sloshed around, but it was not yet high enough to knock out the engine. Peter hurried back up and looked out on deck. Gary was now well behind the boat and drifting off quickly. Peter grabbed the wheel and punched the throttle, taking the risk of turning the boat without trying to time the maneuver.

More water flooded through the broken windshield, but Peter managed to make the turn and get the boat within twenty-five feet of Gary, who still floated motionlessly, a dazed expression still on his face.

Sarge knew that this was his best chance to reach Gary with the line, and this time he waited until the wind would aid him in his throw. He hurled the line out and it fell directly across Gary's shoulder.

Gary made no move to grab the line. He may have been stunned from being hurled through the wall or he may have broken his back.

Sarge and Brad watched in horror as the line slipped off Gary's shoulder, and another wave carried him out of sight.

"Turn! Turn again!" Sarge shouted to Peter, motioning with his hand. Once more Peter punched the engine and made the turn, but this time around there was no sign of Gary.

Peter stepped from the wheel and shouted through the back opening of the pilothouse, "Get your survival suits on!"

Brad and Sarge scrambled into the pilothouse just as a wave struck the boat broadside, sending the *Sea Fever* scudding along the breaking face and again driving the starboard side downward.

When she came back up, Peter got on the radio: "Mayday! Mayday! Mayday! This is the *Sea Fever*! We have lost a man overboard! We are at the 13,250 line just above Powell!"

Peter had given the LORAN-C line and also referred to his position north of Powell Canyon. He knew that Grant Moore on the *Broadbill* and his father in the *Sea Star* were nearby, and he also assumed Billy Garnos of the *Fair Wind* remained in the vicinity. Peter waited for an agonizing second, praying that the radio was still working properly in spite of being soaked with water.

Almost immediately Grant responded. "Peter, we're on our way! Keep talking!"

"Gary's gone, we can't find him! The boat is flooding, she might go down any minute! We've got to get off, she won't stay up much longer!"

A new voice broke in on the radio. "Peter, listen to me! Stay with that boat! Your best chance is with the boat!" It was Bob Brown. "We got problems of our own here, and can't make the turn, so just hang on until Grant gets there!"

Grant's voice returned. "Peter, we will be there soon! I've told the Coast Guard what happened! A cutter is on its way, so hang on!"

Grant did not have the heart to tell Peter that it would take a cutter close to twelve hours to reach the scene and that with the hurricane winds a helicopter was out of the question. And as Grant steered the *Broadbill* into the seas and toward the accident scene, he wondered how he would ever find the *Sea Fever*.

PART II

PART II

CHAPTER 11

Stay with the Boat!

O F ALL THE MARINERS TRAPPED ON GEORGES BANK, Bob Brown was the most experienced. He was forty-three years old and he'd been fishing commercially since he was fourteen, the year he bought a used skiff from which he caught lobsters along the north shore of Massachusetts. Bob worked his way through larger boats and at age thirty he began fishing Georges Bank. On the day of the storm he was captaining the 70-foot *Sea Star* near Corsair Canyon, located approximately twenty miles east-northeast of the *Sea Fever*'s position.

Incredibly, early in the morning when the storm had been blowing 50 knots and the seas were fifteen to twenty feet, Bob Brown had ordered his crew to haul several traps they had previously dropped. His crew must have wondered if he was homicidal as waves washed over the deck and the pilothouse filled with water three separate times. One of those crewmembers was Mike Sosnowski, the deck boss of the *Sea Star*, and a three-year employee of Bob Brown. "I was probably the only crewmember on the boat that wasn't shocked when Bob had us hauling gear, because once that man got on the fishing grounds, he was there to stay. That was my third year working on the *Sea Star*, and I had become almost numb to the crazy risks Bob took. And that morning was awful. I remember shouting at a crewmate who was just a foot away, but he couldn't hear a thing I said over the roaring of the wind."

At about 8 a.m. Bob finally called in the crew, turned the *Sea Star* into the wind, and prepared to ride out the storm. Like the other captains, he couldn't believe the weather forecast could have been so wrong the night before. When the 5 a.m. report called for gale warnings, Bob felt the conditions warranted a storm rating, and when he heard the 11 a.m. revised forecast with its storm warning, Bob thought they should have been issuing hurricane alerts.

Whether he was in a hurricane or a storm, Bob was probably the only man on Georges Bank that day who did not feel the cold grip of trepidation. He had survived storms with winds of 80 knots, but even he marveled at how suddenly this storm arose. While his crew considered donning survival suits and some prayed for their safety, Bob Brown took pictures of the waves. He experienced the storm in an almost detached manner, interested in how his boat would perform and eager to learn from the event. The storm was a formidable challenge to be sure, but not something to fear. He simply could not be intimidated by the ocean, even in the face of seventy-foot seas. Bob found the experience fascinating, feeling a sense of pride that his boat was handling seas larger than many mariners believed possible.

Then he heard the Mayday call from Peter. The wonder of watching the storm gave way to anger because he knew he could not immediately go to his son's aid. It was simply impossible to make any progress going into the teeth of the wind and waves. All he could do was shout to his son on the radio, "Stay with the boat! Your best chance is with the boat!"

Fortunately, however, Grant Moore on the *Broadbill* was west of Peter, and he had the waves mostly at his back as he headed toward the foundering *Sea Fever*.

Grant was of lean build with brown hair and intelligent blue eyes. The twenty-five-year-old had a direct manner and a maturity beyond his years. Like the other fishermen, he had Popeye forearms from lifting trap after trap and was not the kind of person you'd pick a fight with. He was friendly with Peter and had tremendous respect for Bob. His relationship with Bob had started out on the right foot when Bob offered Grant sound advice about lobster fishing on Georges Bank. One day, however, Grant found some of his gear destroyed and he confronted Bob, suspecting Bob had damaged the gear because it was in an area he thought of as his own. Bob told Grant that's exactly what happened and he'd better stay the hell out of that area. Grant responded by saying, "If you ever fuck with me again you'll regret it. Next time talk with me face-to-face."

Surprisingly the two men put this incident behind them and over the years they developed a friendship and mutual respect. "The reason I had such a good relationship with Bob," says Grant, "is probably because I never had to work for him. Instead we had our own boats and occasionally even shared information, such as when Bob gave me tips on adding refrigeration to another boat I bought."

The *Broadbill* was a 65-foot steel lobster boat with a crew of four besides Grant. The crew had hauled gear all day Friday and then into the night. Around 1 a.m. on Saturday morning they had to knock off because it started raining so hard they couldn't find the high-flyers marking the traps. "After we stopped hauling gear," recalls Grant, "one of the crew took watch while I got some rest. About five a.m. the crewmember on watch woke me up and said, 'Grant, you better come look at this.' I went to the pilothouse and immediately knew why he got me up. The seas were really building and during the course of the night we had drifted southeast off the Bank and into fourteen hundred fathoms. I thought it would be better if we were in about fifty fathoms, so I told the guys to secure the boat and take the scuppers out. Then we headed northwest and got back on the Bank not far from Lydonia Canyon to wait out the storm."

When the Mayday call came in around noon, Grant had trouble hearing it through all the static. But there was no mistaking Peter's voice. Grant had talked with Peter a couple of times that morning as well as with Billy Garnos on the *Fair Wind,* and he had a fair idea of Peter's location. He stayed on the radio until he got the exact location of the *Sea Fever,* and then told Peter he was on his way.

"Thank God," says Grant, "that we were not to Peter's south or east, because we could not have made any headway at all going into those seas. It was scary as hell trying to get to him and I knew I was putting my crew at risk, but Peter would have done the same for us. We were taking the seas on our port-stern and we were running as fast as we could. I had a couple guys just looking out at the incoming waves, and had them holler if they saw a really big one, then I'd turn into it. After it went by we'd get back on track. It was the worst weather any of us had ever seen. The *Broadbill* was making sounds we'd never even heard before. And the wind going through the rigging made a screaming noise that I'll never forget. Our pilothouse windows had a little visor over them and as the waves came at us we couldn't see their tops. They were absolute mountains."

Grant radioed the Coast Guard to make sure they had heard Peter's Mayday, which they had. But the nearest cutter was the *Active,* more than 150 miles away, and helicopters could not fly into the 100-mile-an-hour winds tearing over the Bank. The only boat that could help the *Sea Fever* was the *Broadbill,* and Grant wondered if his 65-foot vessel—just 15 feet longer than the *Sea Fever*—could make it to Peter without becoming another casualty of the storm.

Grant's concern was well founded. Throughout maritime history rescuers have often needed rescuing. Getting caught in a storm where the captain must hold position with bow into the seas is bad enough; trying to get from point A to point B in such a storm is much worse, because it puts additional stress on every component of the boat as the seas pound the vessel from new angles. The risks rise further when a captain increases speed to reach a vessel in distress before time runs out. Only nine months earlier, on February 7, 1980, the *Hattie Rose,* a 70-foot steel-hulled fishing trawler just three years old, faced precisely this risk. Captained by twenty-five-year-old Anthony Militello, and laden with fifty thousand pounds of fish that had just been caught at Georges Bank, the *Hattie Rose* was steaming slowly toward its home port of Gloucester, Massachusetts, in snowy, stormy conditions that were deteriorating by the minute. Suddenly a distress call came over the radio; "*Mayday! Mayday! Mayday! This is the fishing vessel* Mother and Grace! *We need immediate assistance!*" Militello instantly responded by altering course and heading toward the struggling vessel, which was about ten miles to his north not far from the tip of Cape Cod. Two other fishing boats, as well as the Coast Guard cutter *Cape Horn,* raced to the foundering vessel.

Waves ranged from twenty to twenty-five feet, with a few topping thirty feet, and the *Hattie Rose* took a terrific pounding as Militello kept the boat on course toward the Mayday call. About thirty minutes into the rescue trip, Militello noticed that his own boat was not responding as it usually did, feeling sluggish as it climbed the cresting seas. He handed the wheel to a crewmember, ran to the back of the pilothouse, and opened the door overlooking the aft deck. What Militello saw horrified him.

The *Hattie Rose*'s stern had sunk so low in the water that waves continuously swept over the deck, and Militello instantly knew why the boat was sluggish: water had found its way down into the bilge. He screamed to his crew to activate all pumps, but it was soon apparent that they could not keep up with the rising water. Now Militello was the one who needed rescuing, and he broadcast his own Mayday before instructing his crew to put on their survival suits.

Fortunately, the Coast Guard cutter *Cape Horn* had just heard from the original boat in distress that its problem was resolved, and another fishing vessel was escorting it to port. Lieutenant Bill Ross on the *Cape Horn* immediately changed the cutter's direction and headed toward the *Hattie Rose,* letting Militello know he was just seven miles away. Ross knew that with winds in excess of 70 miles per hour it would be suicide for a helicopter to launch, and an airlift would be out of the question, leaving the cutter as the sole source of salvation. He decided, however, not to tell Militello of this news, as he didn't want the crew to panic.

After just thirty minutes the *Cape Horn* reached the *Hattie Rose.* Ross had to keep his cutter a safe distance from the sinking vessel to avoid a collision in such violent seas. Ross knew a vessel-to-vessel transfer of the fishing crew would have disastrous results and he radioed his regional rescue commander to discuss his options. The commander suggested firing a line to the *Hattie Rose* so that the fishing boat crew could then pull over a thick line called a towing hawser. But Ross knew that this would be next to impossible. "The weather conditions here," said Ross to his commander, "are such that I don't know if they can even get anyone on deck to catch it because their stern is under."

About this time another fishing boat, the *Paul and Dominic,* arrived at the scene and offered whatever help it could give. The skipper of this third boat trailed behind the other two, ready to snatch men out of the water if the *Hattie Rose* capsized. He radioed Militello to let him know he was standing by and asked how the pumps were handling the incoming water. Militello replied: "We can't get the pumps running. The deck . . . we can't clear the deck and we don't know what's flooded: our water tank, our lazarette, the fish hold—I don't know. Basically the only thing that's not flooded is the engine room. I have everybody up here so I can keep track of everybody. I can't clear the deck. I got to tell you though, we're being swamped!"

To keep the vessel afloat, Militello ran with the wind because the engine room was in the forward part of the boat and he wanted to keep that from being swamped. Each wave threatened to roll the boat, and the crew decided to deploy the life raft, but as soon as the raft inflated, the wind snatched it from their hands and sent it careening into the freezing night. Militello's options were running out and Ross could hear the despair in the captain's voice over the radio. Ross tried to bolster Militello's resolve, saying, "Listen, Cap, you just stay with her. She's, uh, she's still floating . . . just stay with her and maybe, uh, it will work out and you'll be home real quick. Keep all your people together. Gather all the flares and lights and whatever you got here and we're going to stick with you, and if you go in the water we're going to pick you up just as fast as we can."

As the tense minutes grew to an hour, the *Hattie Rose* was blown within two miles of the breaking surf on the back side of Cape Cod. Militello radioed Ross: "Ah, our stern is completely swamped. Jesus Christ, I don't want to risk it any longer. I am scared to risk it, but I don't know, Cap. I don't know if we should jump over the side or not! How long is this helicopter going to take?"

Militello's fear was understandable. If he stayed with the boat it would be crushed like a beer can when it got swept into the shoals closer to shore, a treacherous area of the Cape where countless other mariners have lost their lives. Yet jumping in the water presented its own risks, namely, would the Coast Guard crew on the *Cape Horn* be able to find six men in the pitch-black, snow-filled night in twenty-five-foot seas? Getting lifted off by helicopter seemed much more appealing to the crew of the *Hattie Rose*.

Of course, there was no helicopter on the way, and Ross began steering the conversation with Militello toward the fact that they would probably have to do this rescue on their own with the men jumping off the boat before it capsized. Even though Ross was trailing just seventy-five feet behind the *Hattie Rose*, the seas were so large the two vessels were often out of sight of each other, particularly when both were down in two different wave troughs separated by a wall of water two stories high. At one point a panicky Militello shouted, "Where'd you go, Cap!" Ross replied, "I'm right here behind you, about a ship's length!"

Next, Militello asked Ross to pull alongside him so the men could jump to the cargo net on the cutter. But the seas were still too dangerous and Ross slowly crafted his response: "Ah, I just, I can't put the ship alongside of her. I can't come alongside and take you off. She'll puncture the hull and we'll both go down. I just can't do that, so we're going to have to get as close as we can, throw you lines, and pick you up that way."

Militello and crew were near the breaking point, and he shouted, "Cap, she's all flooded! If we go over the side now we're going to be lost. Twenty-foot seas—you're never going to get us!"

The captain of the *Paul and Dominic* interjected encouragement: "Stay together, jot up the line, and jump off together. You stay tied up to the line together. We'll get you, don't worry about it!"

Meanwhile, Ross maneuvered the *Cape Horn* to within thirty feet of the sinking boat and shot a line over to Militello's crew, who were all tied together. "OK," hollered Ross into the radio mike, "you guys got to think about doing this now!"

Militello agreed. "Cap, when I say go, I'm going to shut the engine down and jump with the guys. You got that, Cap?"

A couple minutes later the *Hattie Rose* suddenly started to roll completely over, and the men did what they had been dreading, hurling themselves into the black seas.

The crew of *Cape Horn* started to pull on the line attached to the men, hauling them toward the cutter with its cargo net hanging over the side. Just as the six men were pulled to within a dozen feet of the cutter, the line snapped. Four men were able to grab a second line thrown to them and then cling to the cargo net where boatswain's mate Duncan Grant and seaman Thomas Jennings were waiting to help them climb up the side of the rolling cutter.

Two men still remained in the surging seas: Militello and his fifty-six-year-old uncle Giacomo Ferrara. They had managed to swim to the cargo net, but Ferrara was so exhausted he couldn't hold on and began drifting away. Militello, who just minutes earlier was terrified of jumping into the seas, risked his own life by letting go of the net and swimming after his uncle, who had been pushed back toward the overturned *Hattie Rose*. For a few moments Ross and the crew aboard the *Cape Horn* lost sight of the two men, and frantically swept their spotlight over the frothing seas.

Five minutes passed. Then, with the help of the crew on the *Paul and Dominic,* Ross located Militello and his uncle surfacing from a wave that had driven them under near the *Hattie Rose.* Ross had to make a quick and difficult decision, knowing he only had a moment to act before the men might be swept out of sight. He maneuvered his cutter between the men, who were upwind, and the overturned vessel, which was downwind, cognizant that his vessel might collide with the *Hattie Rose* or kill Militello and his uncle with the cutter's propeller.

Ross held his breath as well as the cutter's position, which was now beam to the windswept waves. He hoped the seas would push the two drowning men to the cargo net on the cutter, which is exactly what happened. Jennings and Grant once again climbed over the cutter's rail, descended the net, and waited for the men to drift within reach. This time they grabbed the two men and hauled them aboard.

Now, during the height of the November storm at Georges Bank, Grant Moore pushed the 65-foot *Broadbill* as fast as he dared in seas more than twice the size of those that Militello and Ross had faced, and he was well aware that in the span of a second he could switch from potential rescuer to victim. Should something go wrong—such as springing a hatch, catching a wave broadside, or being hit by a rogue wave—it would be disastrous, as there were no other boats in the vicinity to come to his aid.

Although Grant was just fifteen miles from Peter and the *Sea Fever* when he first heard the Mayday, an hour had gone by and he was still five miles away. Every ten to fifteen minutes he radioed Peter to hang on, that he and his crew were making progress but the seas made the going slow. In the back of Grant's mind he struggled with two bleak questions: What are we going to do when we get there and what will we find? He was amazed that the *Sea Fever,* with a third of its pilothouse blown away and in splinters, had not capsized. Even if the boat was afloat when he arrived, Grant already knew a vessel-to-vessel transfer of the crew was out of the question. Like Lieutenant Ross on the *Cape Horn* during his rescue of the *Hattie Rose,* Grant had limited options. There were several differences between the two situations, however, and most of them were not in Grant's favor. The *Broadbill* was nowhere near the size of the 210-foot Coast Guard cutter, nor did it have the rescue equipment found on board a cutter. Grant also faced wind and waves so powerful he wasn't sure he'd be able to maneuver the *Broadbill* when he got to the scene. Unlike Ross, however, at least Grant was operating during the daytime. Thanks to the light, Grant figured that by using his radio he and Peter would be able to locate each other relatively quickly once he arrived in the vicinity of the crippled boat.

The situation, however, did not play out that way. "When we got to where Peter was supposed to be," recalled Grant, "we couldn't see the *Sea Fever* anywhere. We kept shouting into the radio, 'Give us your position again!' We should have been right near them and I'm thinking, Where the hell are they? Then we were coming down off a wave and there they were, right below us!" To this day Grant doesn't know how he managed to avoid slamming into the *Sea Fever,* but somehow the *Broadbill* cleared Peter's boat by a couple of feet.

Now Grant would have to make a dangerous turn. While he waited for just the right moment to make the maneuver, he once again asked himself how he was going to get the *Sea Fever* crew safely aboard his boat.

CHAPTER 12

Tumbling in the Void

THE MEN STILL ALIVE ON THE *SEA FEVER* HAD TWO things going for them that Ernie did not: they had one another and help was on the way. Ernie, on the other hand, floating in the raft, remained utterly alone, and no one even knew the *Fair Wind* had pitch-poled. Although the *Fair Wind* was equipped with an emergency position-indicating rescue beacon (EPIRB), it apparently failed to send a signal. The vessel's EPIRB may have needed to be manually activated or, if it did send a signal, the distress call was never heard. In 1980 the device was still in its infancy and often failed to activate during accidents. At that time the technology relied on aircraft to pick up the signal, rather than satellites, as it does today. The modern EPIRB, called the "406" because it operates on the 406 MHz frequency, sends a signal that can be instantly identified through an encoded transmission program run by the National Oceanic and Atmospheric Administration. Vital information regarding the vessel and its location is passed to the Coast Guard within minutes of its activation, and the EPIRB has a homing device so that rescue aircraft can pinpoint it, even on a drifting boat. If Ernie's ordeal occurred today, he would likely be rescued within hours. That day, however, neither the Coast Guard nor the other boats on the Bank realized the *Fair Wind* had capsized. Of course, Ernie didn't know if the EPIRB on the *Fair Wind* had sent a signal or not. Nor did he dwell on it, because he was fighting for survival on a minute-by-minute basis, simply trying to make correct decisions as each new obstacle was thrown at him.

Now, at approximately 1 p.m., Ernie huddled inside the raft, still tethered to the *Fair Wind*. Chilled to the bone, he continued to endure the onslaught of breaking waves as the 100-mile-per-hour winds shrieked overhead and the wind-raked ocean thundered and roared. It was as if the sea were a living, breathing thing, enraged that one of the *Fair Wind*'s crew had escaped its watery grave and was now bent on claiming Ernie one way or another.

As terrifying as the waves were, Ernie's bigger concern was that the *Fair Wind* would suddenly sink, dragging the raft to the bottom of the sea. The tether connecting the raft to the boat was designed to break free if the boat sank, but Ernie didn't know that, nor was there any guarantee that the line would perform as designed. He knew only that the line was very secure because it had not yet parted from the boat even with all the yanking by the wind and waves.

Approximately forty-five minutes after Ernie first climbed into the raft, he noticed that the *Fair Wind* had settled much lower in the water and only a small section of its hull was visible. Yet still he hesitated to release the raft. Even if his crewmates were dead—a reality that he was coming reluctantly to accept—he wondered if unfastening the raft was the right thing to do. To set himself loose from the boat was a huge decision, because he knew all too well that once the raft became free, it would immediately be carried away from the boat, taking him into the void of endless gray ocean. The raft was equipped with a small paddle, but he knew it would be useless as long as the storm raged.

Ernie's mind raced, churning like the seas around him. The boat had taken on the same significance as the bucket he had clung to earlier—it represented a bit of security, something from his past, something before this misery—and he didn't want to let it go. Maybe the boat will stay up a little longer, he thought, I've always heard to stay with the boat as long as possible. Once again he peered outside at the *Fair Wind*. Now the hull had nearly vanished. Ernie could not postpone the inevitable any longer, and he forced his fingers to untie the bowline knot.

Released from the *Fair Wind*, Ernie was met with a terrifying new sensation. The high, jagged waves instantly snatched the raft, lifting it up and over the wave crests and spinning it from side to side. Sometimes the raft couldn't make it over the waves, but instead went halfway up before the top of the wave caved in on itself, burying the raft under tons of water. The breaking seas smacked Ernie's head and back, sending him sprawling facedown on the floor of the raft. Amazingly, despite the nonstop frenetic motion, he did not get seasick.

Ernie's immediate concern was how to brace himself for the waves that continually struck the raft; he worried their force could break his back. He tried lying on the floor, spread-eagle, as well as sitting with his feet out in front of him and his arms held toward the sides of the canopy. He was still experimenting with different positions when disaster struck. A wave slammed the raft with such fury that it knocked the raft on its side, and Ernie felt himself thrown free from his life-saving capsule. He was now underwater, totally disoriented, and desperate for air. Opening his eyes, he saw the surface above him, and he furiously kicked his way up. He emerged in the foam bare-chested, the wave having ripped away his sweatshirt. Fortunately, the raft was just a few feet away, and Ernie swam with every ounce of strength to reach it before the next wave broke upon him. He clawed his way into the doorway and collapsed on the floor, shaking. Hearing the roar of another wave bearing down on him, he positioned himself as best he could, determined to stay in the raft. Two straps inside walls of the raft served as handholds, and with a viselike grip he vowed not to let go. He even considered trying to somehow lash himself to the tiny vessel but quickly dismissed the idea, worried that if the raft tipped over completely he would drown inside. Ernie didn't know how much more he could take, but he was not going to let it end without fighting back. I may die, he thought, but I'm not going to help it along. As long as this raft floats, I'm staying with it.

Losing his sweatshirt was yet another blow. Although it was soaking wet, it had provided an extra layer between Ernie's body and the seas, helping to trap a small amount of body heat, which would now dissipate immediately. A foot of water was sloshing inside the raft, and Ernie sat with his back against the canopy wall, facing the doorway, with his legs spread in front of him. He couldn't help but wonder how long the raft would hold up against the onslaught. How long would it be before one of the air chambers ripped and sprang a leak? As soon as that thought entered his consciousness, he forced himself to forget it, to just be ready for whatever happened next. He had to focus on what he could control, and that was himself. He could not dwell on the countless ways he might meet his end, but instead told himself, Fight, you son of a bitch, hang in there. Just a few more hours and this storm will have moved on. Then the *Sea Fever* or the *Broadbill* will find me. And if not them, then the Coast Guard will have planes looking for me. It was probably fortunate that Ernie didn't know about the *Sea Fever*'s own desperate situation.

Two hours had passed since the accident, and Ernie had been in the storm so long that he barely noticed the shriek of the wind or the roar of the waves—but he felt their every move, and he tried leaning one way, then another to keep the raft as stable as possible. He was learning to react to the waves, to anticipate their impact and brace himself as much as possible. Holding on to the straps proved exhausting, and he noticed that his fingers had gone numb and cramped. Those hands, so strong from hauling gear all year, felt like rigid claws from his nonstop stranglehold on the straps.

Just a few minutes after Ernie reentered the raft, terror struck again. As he rose to the top of a huge charging wave, the wind caught the raft at just the right angle and sent it tumbling like a paper bag blown over an empty parking lot. The raft careened down the wave and came to rest upside down with Ernie still inside. The small space that had saved Ernie's life now entombed him, just as the *Fair Wind* had when it pitch-poled. Once again he found himself in darkness, underwater, with barely any air in his lungs. And, as before, his brain was screaming, *Get out, get out!* He immediately began to use his hands to grope the sides of the canopy until he found the opening and swam out. Surfacing next to the overturned raft, coughing and spitting up seawater into his dripping black beard, he grabbed at the raft's bottom and hung on to the ballast bag as the seas crashed down on him.

Now that the raft was upside down, its living space was filled with water and acted as a ballast of its own, keeping the raft in that inverted position. Ernie had a sickening feeling that the raft would never right itself, and he knew he no longer had the strength to turn it on his own. Such an effort might cause him to lose his grip, and without the little life-saving capsule, the waves and frigid water would make short work of Ernie, dragging him down into the abyss of an uncaring sea.

As the waves tore at the overturned raft, Ernie mustered a bit of strength and crawled onto the bottom. Although his body was now mostly out of the water, his flesh, raw and red, was exposed to the hurricane force winds and spray. His hands were almost completely numb and what was left of their gripping power weakened with each passing minute. He longed to put his hands under his armpits to warm them a bit, but he dared not let go of the raft. Eying the collapsed ballast bag next to him, Ernie snaked his way inside and squirmed into the fetal position. The bag was partially filled with water, but it shielded him from the wind, and provided a relatively secure place to stay with the raft for whatever the seas had in store for him next.

A tear in the raft's ballast bag likely caused the raft to overturn. Ernie's concern for his friends inside the overturned *Fair Wind* and his reluctance to set the raft adrift meant that the raft remained tethered to the boat for almost an hour, with constant yanking on the lanyard line, which may have ripped the ballast bag. Or perhaps it was the sheer size of the seas that damaged the raft. Whatever the cause, the ballast bag, designed to keep the raft in an upright position, was slightly torn, and when the storm knocked the raft on its side, water escaped from the bag through this tear.

Still, the Givens raft was arguably the best life raft on the market at that time. Upon inflation, other life rafts, without the unique ballast bag, would have become airborne like a kite on a string until the wind ripped them to shreds. The raft that had so far saved Ernie from the seas was the invention of James A. Givens of Tiverton, Rhode Island. Givens came up with the idea for the unique ballast bag while serving in Korea as a paratrooper. "I met several fighter pilots whose buddies had died after ditching in the sea because their raft kept turning over. On my next jump, I looked up at my parachute and thought, I don't know why there couldn't be one of these at the bottom of a life raft." After his hitch in the service was up, Givens bounced around from job to job and even prospected for gold in California, but he couldn't escape the idea of a raft with an inverted parachute at the bottom. His goal to create an "unflippable" raft became an obsession. For years Givens sketched various designs of the raft's mechanical components, making dozens of revisions and testing his invention of a flapper valve located at the very bottom of the ballast bag, which would allow water in but not out.

It wasn't until 1974 that Givens finally produced and sold his first raft, and orders for more quickly followed. "I didn't go to Harvard," said Givens, "and I'm not polished, but what I'm doing is right."

Givens's determination to make and market the safest life raft possible was one reason Ernie was still alive, but the writhing sea and its hammering waves seemed intent on breaching the raft's thin fabric walls.

Despite everything Ernie had gone through, he responded to each new horror with controlled action rather than panic. He focused on the reality of his situation—not what might or might not happen—and reacted to each new peril as intelligently as he could. In a curious way, his boyhood made him better able to cope with the situation. He had not been coddled as a child, and that spurred his independence, just as his toughness likely grew from a childhood without many material possessions. Living in the back of a gas station for a few months as a teenager had given him a lesson in autonomy and street smarts far beyond his years. His stint in the army added to his self-confidence, as did his solo bike ride down the length of the West Coast. Despite the fact that he never went to college, he was a problem solver with a curious mind.

Now, as before, he took advantage of what the situation offered—in this case the shelter of the torn ballast bag.

CHAPTER 13

Inside a Punching Bag

I N MILE AFTER ENDLESS MILE OF STORM-TOSSED OCEAN, Ernie's orange life raft was the only speck of color. It was as if he had been kidnapped, put inside a capsule, and shot into space. No one even knew the *Fair Wind* had run into trouble because Billy had not been allowed any time to send a Mayday, and no one knew Ernie had fought to survive yet was now in desperate need of help. The *Fair Wind* was not scheduled to return to port for another four or five days, and perhaps nobody would become alarmed until it was overdue. By then it would be too late. If Ernie was never found, his friends and family would think it had ended quickly for him, never knowing about his courageous struggle.

For Ernie, the previous two hours had seemed almost as long as his entire prior life. The raft was upside down with Ernie curled up in the ballast bag and both he and the raft were taking a tremendous pounding. It was almost as if Ernie was inside a punching bag being slugged by a giant, unseen fist. Ernie couldn't throw a punch back, so he had taken the only strategy available: outlast his opponent.

He was shivering uncontrollably, and involuntarily tightened his arms around his knees each time a new wave was about to strike. The wait between each wave was about twenty seconds. Most of the waves were uniform in power and height, but every now and then a much stronger one came barreling toward Ernie. It was just such a wave that now lifted the raft up toward its crest and then collapsed on it.

Now Ernie was trapped beneath the raft inside the fully submerged ballast bag, with only seconds to escape before the next wave buried him deeper. He fought his way free, kicked to the surface, and yet again crawled inside the raft's protective shell. Gasping for air, eyes stinging, and freezing to the point of numbness, Ernie did not curse, but instead considered himself fortunate that the raft had righted itself without throwing him aside. He willed his body to get back into a sitting position with his legs spread toward the doorway.

He was on a roller coaster that could not be shut off, the seas taking him sixty feet up, then sixty feet down, mountains and valleys, mountains and valleys. As the raft slid up and over each wave, Ernie experimented leaning one way and then the other, slowly getting the hang of actually controlling the raft a bit so that the doorway faced away from the onrushing seas. Continually drenched, he found this little bit of steering helped to keep new water from coming inside. Between waves he bailed with his hands or with the raft's small paddle, as much to keep his circulation moving as to rid the raft of some of the water. Shivering, he thought about the sweatshirt he had lost and the coat he had discarded in his effort to keep his head above the foam and waves when the *Fair Wind* first pitch-poled.

The winds were still screaming out of the northwest at velocities just better than 100 miles per hour, propelling Ernie southeast, toward the edge of the continental shelf. The *Fair Wind* had gone down in approximately 60 fathoms of water and Ernie was being carried toward Munson Canyon, where the top of the northernmost canyon wall was 137 fathoms deep and the canyon itself abruptly plunged to a depth of 760 fathoms and continued dropping to more than 1,000 fathoms. Because the winds were coming out of the northwest, Ernie knew he was being pushed toward the edge of Georges Bank, but he had no way of knowing what his drift rate was. He hoped it was slower than it felt. He knew that the farther he drifted from the *Fair Wind*'s last position, the harder it would be for rescuers to find him. He still held out hope that the EPIRB had gone off, and that Peter on the *Sea Fever* would come searching. One thing he knew for sure was that Billy never made a Mayday call.

Although Ernie did his best to keep the raft's doorway from facing the oncoming waves, water continued to pour into the tiny craft, so much so that Ernie considered tying the door flap shut. But if I do that, he thought, I might not be able to get out if it flips upside down again. He weighed the pros and cons of this action, just as he had when he considered lashing himself to the inside of the raft, and again he came to the conclusion that he needed the option of swimming free should the raft capsize again. It was ironic that the very raft designed to save him could also drown him. He could even die in the raft while it was right side up—a single wave, if it crashed directly on his head, could knock him out. He'd likely drown in the foot of water at the bottom of the raft.

Just as Ernie thought he was doing a better job of controlling the raft and keeping its door away from the onslaught, an enormous wave lifted the vessel, then crashed down on it, smothering the raft. Ernie, spread-eagle inside, felt himself being pushed upside down, and was suspended that way for a long second. But the raft continued turning, completing a 360-degree roll. Ernie came up coughing and hacking but he was still inside the tiny vessel.

Each wave was taking its toll as he braced himself for the next one, never knowing if it would be the one that would tear the raft apart. His body had been producing adrenaline almost non-stop since the *Fair Wind* pitch-poled, and it was a wonder he hadn't given up from pure exhaustion. Ernie was no more than a tiny cork in the ocean, but a single-minded cork whose primary thought was just to survive the next wave. Every now and then, in the troughs of a wave, he risked shifting position so that he could quickly peek out the doorway, hoping somehow to spot one of the other fishing boats. But he saw only a wall of water so tall it blocked the horizon and muffled the sound of the wind that raged above. Yellow-gray spume flew through the air. He was totally alone.

CHAPTER 14

Trapped

Brad, Sarge, and Peter, still aboard the *Sea Fever*, had adopted a mind-set much like Ernie's: survive the next wave. After losing Gary and issuing the Mayday, the three men donned survival suits and prayed that Captain Grant Moore aboard the *Broadbill* would arrive before the *Sea Fever* went down.

"We were in a real bind," recalls Peter, "because if we tried to go into the seas, the waves would have continued to come through the broken windshield. On the other hand, if we went with the seas, the same surfing and then broaching would happen like when we lost Gary. We knew either one of those positions would get us killed. So we laid to with the engine in neutral because there simply weren't any other options, and we were still afloat. The waves were hitting our port side, which was how we wanted to take them since the starboard side of our pilothouse was in pieces." And so Peter no longer steered the boat, but let the *Sea Fever* be carried sideways by the waves.

Peter didn't know it, but the wooden ribs in the boat's hull were beginning to crack, adding more water to what had already come in through the blown windows and the shattered side of the pilothouse. The pilothouse contained a hand pump, a device that looked somewhat like the kind seen on an old well, and the men took turns working the pump between waves, keeping up with the water collecting in the bilge but never seeming to get ahead of it. A more serious concern than the incoming water, however, was the size of the waves now slamming into and nearly engulfing the boat. Some were so large the men feared being flushed out of the boat through the same shattered opening Gary had crashed through, and they soon abandoned pumping to get into safer positions.

They found that the most secure location was the floor of the pilothouse. They sat with their backs against the port wall and their feet braced against the engine room box, which rose up two feet near the center of the pilothouse. "We would hear each wave coming at us," says Brad, "and the roaring got louder each second. When the wave hit the port side it would tip the boat to an almost ninety-degree angle and we'd be looking straight down at the smashed opening on the starboard side and see a mass of churning water. If our feet lost their grip on the engine room box, we would have been hurled down into that opening and that would be the end. The boat would surf down the breaking wave, and it was just a thunderous, crashing noise, and we would be surrounded by white water. The energy was so strong I really thought the waves would crack the boat like an egg. Then, when the wave passed beneath us, I'd let my breath out, and we would rock back into the trough, the boat would stabilize a bit, and we'd await the next wave. By raising our heads we could see the oncoming wave approach through the port window, and they were as tall as trees. I just had this awful, sinking pit in my stomach watching or hearing the wave approach. And it was physically exhausting trying to keep in the same position. The only thing that kept me going was pure adrenaline coursing through me."

Sarge recalls the harrowing experience with equal clarity. "I really thought that the next big wave was going to knock us so far on our side that we wouldn't come up. And I was worried the radio would die with all the water coming into the boat. Even though Peter got the Mayday off, I wasn't sure Grant would be able to find us. I wanted to get off that boat as quickly as possible, and we talked about what we would do if and when Grant came. We discussed using a rope to tie the three of us in a line so no one would get separated when we went in the water. I was thinking Grant could shoot a line over and haul us through the water with their lobster winch. We all agreed we were going to get off the boat the second Grant arrived." During that agonizing wait for help, Sarge also made a vow that if he lived, the very first thing he would do was go to church. He hadn't been in years, but he thought that should he survive it would be nothing less than a miracle.

Peter feared they were only minutes from death. "The waves put us down to rail level and then just scooted us along at incredible speeds, just like we were going over a waterfall. I remember how we shouted to each other about how we'd tie ourselves together with plenty of line in between us, and then Grant could haul us in. The main thing was that after what had just happened with Gary, we were going to do this together—either we'd all make it or we'd all die. Because we had our survival suits on we even considered not waiting for Grant, and instead jumping over together immediately. That's how certain we were that the boat was going to roll completely over on the next big wave and we'd be trapped inside. But then I remembered my father shouting, 'Stay with the boat no matter what,' so we decided to follow his advice."

Peter couldn't help thinking back to the start of the trip.

Unlike the crew of the *Fair Wind,* Peter had been reluctant to violate the old fisherman's superstition that warned about setting out on a Friday. But he knew his father would never allow a superstition to get in the way of fishing, and so Peter never even mentioned it, and had done his best to ignore it altogether. Now Gary was gone, and Peter and the rest of his crew seemed likely to suffer the same bleak fate at any minute.

Two hours after the *Sea Fever's* terrifying ordeal began, Grant's *Broadbill* finally arrived. The crew of the *Sea Fever* first spotted the *Broadbill* on the crest of a wave high above them, but it soon careened down the face of the wave, nearly plowing into the *Sea Fever.* On the one hand, the crewmen were relieved that Grant had found them, but the sight of Grant's boat made them realize the waves were even taller and more violent than they'd thought, which plunged them into a deeper despair. The ocean tossed the 70-foot *Broadbill* as easily as it would a toy. One second the *Broadbill* would soar high above the *Sea Fever's* crew, its propellers briefly visible in the foam, and the next minute they'd be looking down on the *Broadbill,* spray and rain sweeping over her deck. Still, so desperate were the men on the *Sea Fever,* they considered following through with their plan to jump into the sea.

Peter radioed Grant and shouted that the *Sea Fever* felt like it was about to go down, and they were preparing to jump off. Grant yelled back not to make a move, that he'd swing around and try to get closer, and then they'd figure out what to do. Grant turned the *Broadbill,* but the action proved so violent he radioed Peter again almost immediately, "If you're really going to jump I'll try and get you, but I'm telling you I don't think you're going to make it. We will end up killing you guys. You'll get crushed. Just look at the action of my stern."

Peter knew Grant was right, and so did Sarge and Brad. "I couldn't wait to get off," says Sarge, "but I could see the way the waves were crashing against the hull of the *Broadbill,* and it didn't look good. I thought we might not survive being pulled alongside and instead be killed by slamming into his steel hull. It seemed cruel to have help so close but still be trapped on the boat."

The tension, Brad recalls, was unbearable. "I had put all my hopes into Grant getting us off the boat, and now I could see that might not work. At nineteen years old I was terrified and I just tried to keep my emotions in check, and let Peter and Grant make the right decision. With each wave I'm thinking there's a large chance I'm going to die, and that feeling over and over is just awful. And here was another boat just sixty feet away and yet we couldn't get off. If the *Sea Fever* went all the way over—and it sure felt like it would—there wasn't a thing Grant and his crew could do. We'd die right in front of him, trapped in the pilot-house, where we would be drowned."

CHAPTER 15

Just a Blustery Day

THE STORM THAT HIT GEORGES BANK IN NOVEMBER of 1980 caused little more than blustery autumn winds in Massachusetts, and residents of the state went about their weekend business never realizing that a nightmare was raging not far off the coast. The weekend newscasts focused on the fifty-two U.S. hostages who had been held in Iran since November 1979 and the latest reports coming out of Las Vegas regarding a horrific fire that killed eighty-four people at the MGM Grand Hotel and Casino.

About the only people in New England who knew that a storm of titanic proportions was raging at Georges Bank were those working at the U.S. Coast Guard's regional headquarters in Boston. Throughout the morning Lieutenant Robert Eccles had juggled no fewer than eight search and rescue operations, including four "sinkers." He and his fellow Coasties, as they often call themselves, at the operations center had directed a number of successful rescues without any loss of life; that is, until they received the Mayday from the *Sea Fever*. Eccles now knew that a crewmember had been swept off the boat, and he worried that the remaining crewmembers would not survive long enough for the *Broadbill* or the cutter *Active* to reach them. He alerted Air Station Cape Cod to attempt to send a helicopter to the scene, though he knew the high winds might make it impossible to send one any time soon.

Safe in the confines of his office, Eccles felt a sense of helplessness hearing the details of the emergency without being able to do anything physically to help. During his tenure in the Coast Guard, Eccles had come to the conclusion that talking to people in Mayday situations was often much more draining than being involved in the actual on-scene search and rescue. "There have been times," recalls Eccles, "when I'd be talking to fishermen on the radio, and I knew they were going to die within minutes. One of the worst times was talking to two men aboard a fishing vessel sinking off Gloucester in the winter. They radioed in their Mayday, and I dispatched patrol boats to assist them, but it would take a while for them to reach the fishing boat. The two men said the boat was sinking lower by the second. I asked if they had their life jackets on, and they responded that they did. Then I asked if they had their survival suits on and they said, 'No, they're down below.' That's when I knew I was talking to dead men. It was going to take them a good five minutes or more to get those suits and get them on, and by that time the boat would be submerged. They had to abandon ship immediately, and I knew they wouldn't last in the water more than a few minutes, not nearly long enough for our boats to get there. When our vessels got on site, the fishing boat was gone and so were the men."

Eccles had several years of experience coordinating difficult rescues but nothing had prepared him for the relentless stream of emergencies he was handling that Saturday.

*   *   *

While Ernie and the men aboard the *Sea Fever* struggled to stay alive, their families and loved ones had no idea of their plight. In a sad twist of fate, Maria Pavlis, the fiancée of the *Fair Wind*'s captain, Billy Garnos, was shopping for her wedding dress in Boston at approximately the same time the *Fair Wind* pitchpoled and Billy drowned. Maria had met Billy through his sister in the early 1970s, when Maria was a teacher and Billy had just been drafted into the army and was soon to be sent to Vietnam. Maria had her second-grade students write to Billy, hoping that the letters would make Billy laugh and give him some comfort so far away from home. When Billy returned from Vietnam he continued to be the big-hearted, fun-loving guy he was before he left, and he rarely mentioned Vietnam and didn't volunteer any information about the combat he saw. But some friends knew he'd seen plenty. In fact, one friend, fishing boat captain Hugh Bishop, found out the hard way. Hugh had hired Billy as a deckhand on his 50-foot fishing vessel, the *Mistress,* and they made two-day trips out of Marblehead, line-trawling for ground fish. On one of the overnight trips Hugh went down to wake Billy up for his turn on watch and got quite a surprise. "No sooner did I put my hand on his shoulder," says Hugh, "than Billy grabbed my throat in a vise-like grip. He had come from a dead sleep to having a stranglehold on me in half a second. Billy later explained it was because of what he'd been through in Vietnam. I made sure in the future that when I woke him, I hopped out of reach immediately."

Billy's fiancée, Maria, was similarly convinced of the impact Vietnam had had on Billy. He'd have terrible nightmares and jump out of bed in a sweat. Maria would ask, "Do you want to talk about it?" And Billy would respond, "No, it's better that I just try to forget it." But Billy couldn't forget, and a couple of days before the storm at Georges Bank, he shocked Maria by saying, "When I get back from this next trip, I want to tell you about Vietnam."

Just before the Georges Bank accident, Billy and Maria had gotten engaged. Although they'd known each other for years, they did not connect romantically until the wedding of Billy's sister, Rose, who was a friend of Maria's, on September 6, 1980. "Something magical happened that day. It was as if we had always been together," says Maria. "We were engaged on November 11, 1980, and planned to be married on February 14, 1981. It was such a short time but I had never been happier, and in my heart I know that Billy was just as happy."

Maria knew Billy loved fishing, and she knew its dangers, but never tried to persuade him to find other work. It was clear that fishing gave him a deep sense of satisfaction. Their relationship was built around the fishing trips, and Billy made Maria feel special each time he left port and returned. "Before he'd head to sea," says Maria, "he would order flowers so they would be waiting for me when I got home from work. And then when he returned he'd bring flowers and chocolates, and sometimes lobster for dinner."

Billy also included Maria in his dreams and goals, telling her how much he looked forward to being the captain of the new boat Charlie Raymond was building. He even took Maria down to the waterfront to see the new boat being constructed. "Billy was just so happy and proud," says Maria, "that all his hard work was being recognized by Charlie, and he couldn't wait to captain this bigger boat. I remember he took me on board and showed me around, saying, 'No more fifty-foot *Fair Wind* when this boat is finished.'"

CHAPTER 16

A Silent Killer

ERNIE'S SITUATION HAD CHANGED LITTLE AS THE afternoon progressed and the storm maintained its intensity. Over the course of the day he had swallowed a fair amount of seawater, which only increased his mounting thirst from the exertion required to stay inside the raft. He could see a survival bag tied to the inside walls of the raft, and between waves he glanced inside the bag, noting it contained flares, a pump, cookies, and, most important, six cans of water, but he dared not remove any of the contents from the bag for fear the seas would sweep them out the door. He could go awhile longer without the precious liquid.

Ernie had now been subjected to more than three hours of hell, and the mental strain was unimaginable. In the blink of an eye his world had collapsed. He had lost his friends, his boat, and nearly his life. In an uncaring sea, he was a mere speck in mile after mile of raging white water.

Most people would have cracked under such pressure, but Ernie still focused on each problem as it arose. And there was absolutely no room for error. At each moment when action was called for, he had to get every decision right without discussing his reasoning with anyone else. He was being put through a mental and physical test, where he couldn't score a 98 percent or 99 percent, but instead—to live—had to score 100 percent.

Ernie's teeth were chattering, his lips blue, his flesh waterlogged, and his stamina flagging. The waves assaulting his raft had managed to swallow the 50-foot steel-hulled *Fair Wind*. What chance did he have with only one-eighth of an inch of rubberized fabric separating him from the roaring sea? The seas were unrelenting; it would have been so easy to give up and just slip away, ending the nightmare quickly. But Ernie refused.

At approximately 3 p.m. an especially strong wave ambushed Ernie yet again. Thousands of pounds of surging seawater slammed into his head and back, and tipped the raft on end so that the doorway faced directly downward. With diminished strength, Ernie clutched the canopy straps, holding his breath, while he tried to use his legs to keep from falling through the doorway. Fortunately, the raft continued rolling, completing a 360-degree turn as the rest of the frothing wave slid beneath him. Remarkably, when the raft returned to its upright position, enough water flooded back into the ballast bag to keep the raft from getting rolled by the next chaotic wave, allowing Ernie to get a desperately needed breath of air. Water cascaded out of the raft, leaving only a foot or two sloshing at the bottom, as Ernie steeled himself for the next wave and pushed the canopy top back into place.

In addition to the waves, another enemy was working against Ernie, hypothermia. This silent killer was making inroads against Ernie's body, as he was losing more heat than he could generate. If his body's core temperature declined to 87 degrees, he would lose consciousness and die.

Ernie was now well into the initial stages of hypothermia. His body had begun to shiver violently in an effort to increase body heat. The shivering, however, was having little effect because half of his body was submerged in the 55-degree water sloshing around inside the raft. During the brief lulls between waves he often tried to bail out some of the water using his small paddle, but he could never remove the bottom six or seven inches covering the floor of the raft.

The air temperature at Georges Bank was about the same as the ocean's, but it was the water doing the damage, sucking away Ernie's body heat twenty-five times faster than the air. His extremities suffered most. The blood vessels in his hands and feet were beginning to contract, allowing less blood to flow through them, which in turn reduced the amount of cold blood returning to his vital organs. The body's defense in these conditions is to relinquish the hands and feet to the cold in an effort to concentrate the diminishing warmth in the inner core and the vital organs.

If the hypothermia advanced, blood flow to Ernie's arms and legs would also decrease. The rate of heat loss varies slightly among individuals, primarily due to body fat. Ernie was six feet tall, 195 pounds, and most of that was muscle rather than fat, thanks to his grueling work as a fisherman.

The raft's canopy was probably Ernie's best protection against hypothermia. The canopy's thin fabric helped to shield Ernie from the wind chill, which speeds heat loss from the body. Unfortunately, the canopy was about all Ernie had to aid in his struggle against the cold. Most heat loss occurs through a person's head, and Ernie had no hat. His sweatshirt had been stripped away by the waves, and all he had on was a pair of jeans and socks, but because they were both wet, they retained only a fraction of their insulating value.

Conserving energy is another way to retard the process of heat loss, but Ernie didn't have that luxury, as his more immediate concern was to keep himself in the raft and keep it upright, which required shifting and balancing. Despite all these problems, his situation was brighter than before he entered the raft.

Peter, Sarge, and Brad—still trapped on the *Sea Fever*—had the benefit of survival suits, unlike Ernie. Thanks to these specially designed suits, hypothermia was not an issue for the *Sea Fever* crew, but drowning remained a very real threat. If a wave caught the vessel just right, the port side, which was lifted to an almost 90-degree angle on every wave, would continue all the way over, trapping the men inside. Their predicament would be much like the one faced by the crew of the *Fair Wind* when it pitch-poled. Perhaps the broken windows and shattered starboard pilothouse wall of the *Sea Fever* would offer better escape routes, but the survival suits might hinder their movement. And if the *Sea Fever* capsized, the buoyancy of the survival suits would push the men up against the deck and into a temporary air pocket, from which they would be hard pressed to descend and grope for an opening from the boat.

So far, however, the decision to let the boat lay to without power or steerage and just surf sideways down the waves was working, if just by a matter of inches. Peter could not turn the boat into the seas because the windshields were gone, and he had already tried running in the same direction the waves were traveling, with disastrous consequences. All three men agreed the best course of action was to continue to let the boat ride the liquid mountains on its own. They had to stay in their cramped sitting position with their feet braced against the engine block, or they'd slide into the abyss on the starboard side. In the survival suits, with the mitten hands, it would be impossible to grab anything to stop the slide, and the churning white water outside the boat would likely knock them unconscious against the *Sea Fever's* hull.

Grant Moore, on the *Broadbill,* watched the *Sea Fever* with amazement as the wounded vessel surfed down the face of each towering wave, propelled by a boiling fury of foam and seawater. "I could see how low the *Sea Fever* was riding in the water," says Grant, "but there was nothing we could do except stand off as close as we could. So I put my stern off his bow and just clutched in and out of gear trying to stay as close as possible." Grant's situation was akin to that of an airport traffic controller who is helpless to free passengers from an incoming plane with mechanical trouble. The controller might have a visual on the plane and give advice over the radio, but all he or she can really do to help is order emergency teams and equipment to stand by. In Grant's situation, he had both a visual on the *Sea Fever* and radio communication, and now he stood by, ready to respond if the worst happened.

On the *Sea Fever* the roar of the waves muffled most other sounds but Peter still heard the boat make some noises he'd never heard before. Occasionally the boat would groan as if it were alive and in its final throes of agony, while other times he thought he heard sharp cracks coming from below. Peter strained to listen, wondering if the wooden spine and ribs of the vessel were coming apart faster than he suspected. There was so much gear crashing around below in the galley and bunkroom it was impossible for him to know. To go below could be suicide, because if the boat did turn turtle he'd never escape. "There was nothing we could do now except wait it out," says Peter. "And I don't think Sarge, Brad, and I said more than a few words to each other."

The crew took turns working the manual pump as best they could, then retreated into their grief over losing Gary, coupled with the fear that they would not survive the afternoon. "The waiting was unbearable," says Brad, "just agony, never knowing if the next wave was going to finish us off. I'd put all my hopes into the *Broadbill* saving us and now we had to hang on indefinitely."

CHAPTER 17

A Pilot's Nightmare

H ELICOPTER PILOTS BUCK BALEY AND JOE TOUZIN were exhausted. Throughout the day on Saturday, November 22, 1980, they had flown mission after mission from Air Station Cape Cod at Otis Air National Guard Base to vessels in distress up and down the New England coast. Now, at approximately 4:30 p.m., rescue coordinators determined that the winds over Georges Bank had abated slightly, enough to attempt a helicopter rescue of the men aboard the crippled *Sea Fever*. Baley and Touzin were reaching their limit, and so was their Sikorsky HH-3F "Pelican" twin-engine amphibious helicopter. It didn't help that most of the flight would be made in the evening and at night with no natural light.

"We had a crew of four," says Baley, "and all of us were just beat. We had logged a lot of air time, flying to one case after another near Cape Cod. The trip to Georges Bank had us concerned."

Touzin concurred, adding, "A round-trip to Georges Bank was approximately 325 miles with a half hour allowed for our

on-scene work. We knew we would be at the max of the chopper's fuel limit, so after we left Otis about 4:30 p.m., we made a
brief stop at Nantucket to top off our tanks. After that, as we
headed for Georges Bank, I couldn't help but think about the
crew from Otis that was killed in 1979."

Touzin and Baley had good reason to be concerned. The helicopter accident that lingered in the backs of their minds occurred
under conditions eerily similar to the ones the two pilots now
faced. On February 18, 1979, an H-3 on a night mission from
Air Station Cape Cod crashed into the icy seas of Georges Bank
during a storm. The pilot, Lieutenant Commander James Stiles,
thirty-three, and copilot, Captain George Burge, thirty-eight,
were experienced fliers. Just weeks earlier Stiles had received the
Fineberg Award from the American Helicopter Society for heroism and been named Pilot of the Year. Stiles had previously been
stationed in Kodiak, Alaska, where pilots face some of the worst
flying conditions in the world. There he had been awarded the
Distinguished Flying Cross. Burge, a captain in the Canadian
Forces participating in an exchange program, had logged fourteen
years of flying in all kinds of weather.

Their mission started as a routine one at 9:30 p.m. when a
Japanese fishing vessel, the *Kaisei Maru,* requested that an injured
fisherman be airlifted to the nearest hospital. Stiles and Burge,
along with three other crewmen, immediately took off in their
helicopter heading southeast to pick up the injured man. After
flying for several miles, however, they were called back because
base commanders had pinpointed the *Kaisei Maru*'s exact location
and determined that it was just beyond the chopper's range. The
aircraft returned to base to refuel and wait for the *Kaisei Maru* to
steam closer.

It wasn't until 3:14 a.m. that the same crew was ordered back
to the chopper to complete the mission. The copter arrived on
scene without incident, but conditions had deteriorated. Winds

were gusting to 40 knots, and waves were cresting at thirty feet, throwing spray five hundred feet into the air. To make matters worse, it was snowing. In the back of the helicopter, hospital corpsman Bruce Kaehler, airman electrical technician John Tait, and petty officer Mark Torr readied the rescue basket for lowering, as the chopper circled the fishing vessel.

Once pilot Stiles found the position most favorable for hovering above the vessel, he gave the OK to lower the hoist. Torr and Tait were lowering the basket when suddenly the chopper pitched violently. Mark Torr remembers hearing someone shout, "We're going to hit the water!" Within a matter of one or two seconds the chopper plunged into the frigid seas below. Torr was thrown from the open door, where the hoist had been lowered, and struggled to stay afloat in the crashing seas. The H-3 lay upside down, floating up and over the waves.

The crew of the Japanese fishing boat was able to rescue Torr, and later retrieved the bodies of Stiles, Burge, and Tait. The body of Bruce Kaeler was never recovered.

Coast Guard investigators launched a full inquiry to determine the cause of the crash, with the first order of business to salvage the helicopter for analysis. The Coast Guard cutter *Active* arrived at the crash site within twenty-four hours and attached floating collars to the helicopter to keep it on the surface until a navy vessel with cranes arrived to lift the bird out of the water. Unfortunately, when the USS *Ponce* arrived, the cables holding the helicopter afloat malfunctioned and the chopper sank to the bottom of the ocean, drifting off the continental shelf, too deep for recovery. No one will ever know for sure what caused the calamity, but investigators theorized that either the engines ingested salt water, causing them to fail, or ice formed on the chopper's shell, destabilizing it.

And now another H-3 was heading out to Georges Bank, and wind conditions and wave heights were higher than those faced by the crew that crashed just a year and a half earlier. Pilots Baley and Touzin tried not to think about their friends who died in that accident, but found it impossible. Adding to their concern was a deep weariness from the already hectic day and an uncertainty about what kind of conditions they'd find out at Georges Bank. Although the winds had eased from hurricane force, they'd heard frightening reports about incredible wave heights of seventy feet. All they knew was that the *Sea Fever* had lost a man overboard and the vessel was foundering after having its windows blown out.

"Flying out," says Baley, "we were really watching our fuel gauges, thinking about the return trip. Winds were coming out of the northwest, assisting us on the trip out, but we'd be flying into them on the flight home. We were streaking right along, anxious to make radio contact with the crippled vessel or one of the other fishing vessels that was standing by."

Baley was the aircraft commander for the flight and sat in the pilot's seat on the right side of the helicopter, while Touzin manned the copilot seat. The two men, however, took turns actually piloting the helicopter, a standard practice. Because it was late November, both men worried about icing—the disastrous effects of ice buildup on the rotors. Consequently, they flew the chopper lower than fixed-wing aircrafts would have, hoping to avoid the ice by staying in the relatively warmer temperatures near the ocean's surface. Also on board was navigator Tony Davern, who sat in the back of the chopper and operated the electronic navigation system, LORAN-C, making sure they stayed on course while at the same time staying in contact with Coast Guard Communication Station (Comstat) Boston. Tony described the mission as "task saturated" because the weather was so bad it kept the crew extremely busy, and he made sure he monitored their distance from Nantucket and Long Island as they proceeded. He wanted to know exactly where the nearest point of land was in case of an emergency. A fourth crewmember, whose name could not be recalled, would operate the rescue hoist once they reached the *Sea Fever.*

The closer the H-3 got to the *Sea Fever,* the worse the conditions became, and the wind buffeted the chopper. Neither Baley nor Touzin felt comfortable with the mission, and because they had been flying all day they worried that their reflexes were not as sharp as they should have been. They needed to stretch and to rest, but in the cramped cockpit, surrounded by instrument panels and equipment, they could do neither. Wind gusts frequently pushed the bird off course, and both men worried about their ability to safely rescue men from a sinking boat in such terrific wind. How would they be able to hold a hovering position if they could barely stay in a straight line under full forward power? In the dark, trying to maintain a constant altitude just above the boat, there would be little to no visual reference points for the pilots; they would have to rely heavily on the hoist operator's instructions coming through their headsets. They would need to be low enough for the basket to reach the pitching boat but not so low that the spray from the wave tops could reach their engine.

The hoist operator would have his own problems trying to control a wildly swinging rescue basket at the end of a wire cable. Waves would lift the boat close to the chopper as they crested, but then drop it low in the troughs. All the while, the chopper would be lurching from turbulence. The radio operator would be in the doorway as well, helping the hoist operator and offering another set of eyes alert to danger. Every man on that helicopter would need to operate in a delicate, balanced, and coordinated way to be precise enough to pull off this rescue. And the crew of the *Sea Fever* would need to be as steady and decisive as possible to avoid disaster—if they grabbed for the rescue basket too soon, they might miss and tumble off the boat. And if they failed to get hold of the basket at the right moment, the basket itself might slam into them and knock them overboard. Fishing them out of the water would be next to impossible—the chopper crew would have to lower the basket beneath the water's surface so the victim in the cumbersome survival suit could claw his way into it. At night this was a worst-case scenario, with the real possibility that the pilots and hoist operator would be unable to locate the men in the midst of so much streaking foam and churning seas.

These thoughts raced through the minds of Baley and Touzin. Being cautious is part of what makes a good pilot, just as nervous tension keeps a person focused and alert. Of course, a pilot cannot let this apprehension turn into debilitating fear, which would in turn affect performance. Hours of training and years of actual experience help prevent this outcome. Baley had logged close to two thousand hours of flight time in the Coast Guard, including a two-year tour in Kodiak, Alaska, where he flew many missions with Jim Stiles, the pilot who had died in the 1979 crash at Georges Bank. The rugged, high terrain of the coastline provided additional challenges to night flying. Joe Touzin had Coast Guard flying experience as well as combat seasoning. He had been a captain in the marines, stationed on an aircraft carrier off the coast of Vietnam. In the closing days of that war, Joe flew chopper missions into Saigon to rescue people as the Vietcong and North Vietnamese entered the outskirts of the city. He understood pressure, and that understanding was going to help him in this rescue.

On board the *Sea Fever,* Sarge felt a glimmer of hope that he, Peter, and Brad were going to make it without ending up in the water. Sometime between 4 and 5 p.m. he noticed that the wind outside the pilothouse had decreased somewhat in intensity. The waves were every bit as ferocious as before, but for the first time since 5 a.m. that morning, Sarge felt convinced that the seas would not grow any larger. As night fell around the crippled

On a calm, cold day in November 1980, the *Fair Wind,* a 50-foot steel lobster boat based in Hyannis, Massachusetts, set out for what would be its final voyage. *(Maria Pavlis/Billy Garnos)*

The *Sea Fever,* a 50-foot wooden lobster boat battered and beaten by the ferocious freak storm, was owned by Bob Brown, who later bought the doomed *Andrea Gail,* made famous by Sebastian Junger's *The Perfect Storm. (Peter M. Brown)*

Ernie Hazard, a tough, three-year veteran of the *Fair Wind*'s crew, had never encountered waves as tall or as fierce as those he faced that day. *(Maria Pavlis/Billy Garnos)*

Billy Garnos, the thirty-year-old captain of the *Fair Wind,*
did not believe in taking unnecessary chances. Had he
learned of the looming storm, he almost certainly would
have delayed the trip. *(Maria Pavlis / Billy Garnos)*

Twenty-two-year-old Rob Thayer of the *Fair Wind* was a rookie nearing the end of his first lobster-fishing season. As fate would have it, his first season would also be his last. *(Maria Pavlis/Billy Garnos)*

At just twenty years old, Dave Berry was the youngest member of the *Fair Wind*'s ill-fated crew. *(Nancy Antonich)*

Billy Garnos had recently gotten engaged. As he stepped aboard the *Fair Wind* that November day, he had no reason to suspect that he would never see his young fiancée again. *(Maria Pavlis/Billy Garnos)*

Father and son Bob and Peter Brown were both swept up in the storm; twenty-two-year-old Peter captained the *Sea Fever*, and Bob the *Sea Star*. *(Peter M. Brown)*

Richard Rowell *(center)*, nicknamed "Sarge" by his *Sea Fever* crewmates, was a twenty-one-year-old former marine. *(Peter M. Brown)*

Sarge relished the demanding life of an offshore lobster fisherman, which often called for twenty-hour days spent heaving lobster traps on and off the deck.
(Peter M. Brown)

Among the boats lost in the storm that day was the *Determined,* a 76-foot wooden lobster boat, whose lucky crewmembers were plucked from the sea by the Coast Guard cutter *Active.* *(QM2 Wayne A. Hennessy)*

As the *Active*'s launch boat approached Ernie Hazard's tiny, inflatable raft, rescuers saw no signs of life inside. *(QM2 Wayne A. Hennessy)*

Rescuers from the Coast Guard cutter *Active* wrapped Ernie Hazard in a thick blanket; it was the first dry thing he had touched in fifty hours. *(QM2 Wayne A. Hennessy)*

Although out of the raft and under the care of the Coast Guard, Ernie Hazard remained in peril. His skin was visibly blue, and rescuers worried that his body would go into shock. *(QM2 Wayne A. Hennessy)*

boat, Sarge kept these thoughts to himself. He didn't want to speak too soon. By 6 p.m. he felt confident enough that he shouted to Brad and Peter, asking if they felt the wind had eased a little. They had been thinking the same thing but, like Sarge, were almost afraid that if they said anything too soon, they'd invite more fury from the storm.

Indeed the wind had slackened, but the men were only slightly relieved. Their muscles still tensed each time a new wave slammed the boat, and they wondered if the wooden vessel could continue to hold its own against the seas. So far, however, the boat had saved them from what looked like certain death just three hours earlier. They now realized that the decision to stay inside the *Sea Fever* instead of leaping into the water when the *Broadbill* arrived probably saved them from drowning or getting crushed by the *Broadbill*. And now they were thinking ahead to their next decision—what to do when and if a helicopter arrived.

Peter decided to raise his father on the radio again. He explained their predicament, and again Bob Brown's instructions were the same: to remain on the boat even if a helicopter arrived. He pointed out that the boat had already survived the worst of the storm, and if the *Sea Fever* had lasted this long, it would certainly carry them through the night. Bob had decades of experience on the sea, and he thought this course of action would be the safest. Of course, he also had the *Sea Fever* itself in mind—why abandon a vessel, equipment, and gear worth more than a hundred thousand dollars if they could be saved?

Bob added that just as soon as the size of the waves decreased, he would start pounding his way toward the *Sea Fever,* and he figured he'd be able to arrive sometime after dawn. "Just have the helicopter drop you a pump," Bob shouted into the radio, "and everything is going to be all right."

Peter agreed. They'd been keeping up with the incoming water with the hand pump, and with a backup gasoline-powered pump from the Coast Guard he'd have another line of defense. He talked it over with Brad and Sarge, who also thought staying with the boat was better than trying to grab hold of a swinging rescue basket. With the *Sea Fever* surfing sideways down the waves they knew the helicopter crew would have trouble positioning the basket and the men would have an equally tough time climbing into it. The three men shuddered at the thought of one of them falling from the basket into the blackness below, and that fear was enough to keep them together on the boat.

Peter raised Grant on the radio and told him of the decision. Grant too agreed, saying he'd keep the *Broadbill* just off their bow through the night.

When Joe Touzin, Buck Baley, and Tony Davern were ten miles from the *Sea Fever*, they were able to raise Peter on the radio and were relieved to learn that the crew had decided to stay with the boat. "We asked them if they wanted to get off," says Touzin, "but they elected to stay on board and asked us to lower a pump. That was probably the right decision because there's nothing easy about dropping and retrieving a rescue basket in high seas, strong winds, and at night. Any number of things can go wrong."

As the chopper sped toward the *Sea Fever*, the pilots began to explain to Peter how they would get the pump to the crew below. They could not simply lower the pump at the end of a line; that would swing like a wrecking ball. Instead the hoist operator would tie the pump to one end of a line, and the opposite end of the same line would be weighted. Then as the helo hovered as well as it could over the boat, the hoist operator would drop the weighted end of the line onto the boat, hoping it would land on the open deck behind the pilothouse. One of the crewmen would then have to go out on the deck and retrieve the line, then the helo would enter a low hover and the hoist operator would drop the pump, in a floating watertight canister, into the ocean and the men on the *Sea Fever* could haul the pump in. In theory, and in most situations, the plan was fairly easy to execute. At night, in sixty-foot seas with powerful wind gusts, it was anything but.

The chopper crew could see the *Sea Fever* and the *Broadbill* on their radar whenever the boats came up out of the troughs, and the helicopter arrived at the scene within minutes. At this point, the pilot flew strictly by instruments and the copilot looked out the window until he made visual contact with the boat. Then they flicked on the helicopter's landing gear and searchlight. "We didn't put on our most powerful light, called the 'Night Sun,' " says Baley, "because we didn't want to blind the guys on the boat since they would have to be looking for the rope we were going to drop."

Next, the pilots began coaxing the chopper into a lower position above the *Sea Fever*. "The main thing going through my mind," says Baley, "was that we had to be low enough to be accurate dropping the line but high enough that we didn't get caught by a big sea—that would push the boat's rigging into the helo." Everything was in constant motion—the boat, its rigging, the helicopter, and the seas—making it difficult for the pilots and the hoist operator (who would try to drop the pump's trail line across the stern of the boat) to guide the helicopter and maintain the proper hover position. Tony Davern, the navigator, recalls that the boat was violently pitching and rolling. He worried about the men on board and their decision to stay, but he said to himself, *It's their boat and it's their lives.*

The whirling of the helicopter's main rotor blade was kicking foam into the air, and the pilots worried that the salt spray was entering the engines. The chopper's low hover position combined with the high wind meant that the engines were ingesting a small amount of salt water—not a big deal initially, but over a fairly short period of time, salt deposits build up on the turbine blades on the intake side of the engine. This disrupts the airflow across those blades, and the engines begin to run hotter for a given turbine speed. "If the buildup of salt deposits continues, the airflow is disrupted to the point that the engine basically stalls because not enough air is getting into the combustion chamber, and the temperature goes way up and the power way down," explained Baley. "If in a hover and you're heavy, and this happens, it's very likely you're going in the water." This was likely the fate of the Coast Guard helicopter that had gone down at Georges Banks almost two years earlier. It was therefore imperative that Baley's helicopter hover only briefly, which meant dropping the pump line accurately on the first try.

The hoist operator was responsible for directing the pilots into the perfect position so that he could make the drop. Speaking into the radio transmitter attached to his helmet, the hoist operator said, "Easy left," then "Forward, ten feet." He looked down and could see the stern of the *Sea Fever* directly below. The chopper was pointed into the wind, and he knew the line would be blown backward, so he again instructed the pilots to go forward another few feet. Then he dropped the line.

Sarge recalled how the lights from the helicopter illuminated the towering waves and whitecaps in an eerie glow. "Those Coast Guard guys were real pros," says Sarge. "On the first try they dropped that line right across the boat. I crawled out on the deck and grabbed it. Then they dropped the pump in the water right next to us and all we had to do was haul it in."

The pilots told the men below that they had just enough fuel to get back to Nantucket, but they'd make a quick search for Gary. They turned on their multimillion-candlepower light, the "Night Sun," and started making wider and wider circles around the boat. Baley describes the search as follows: "It's as if you had to look for a silver dollar on a football field at night with a flashlight while riding a moped and you only had a limited amount of time. I won't say it was impossible, because we have found people at night with no reflective tape or strobe lights, but it sure was a long shot."

Down below, Peter, Brad, and Sarge knew Gary was long since dead, and that the pilots would never find him. As the roar of the helicopter's engine and the thumping of its rotors faded and was replaced by the hissing, growling seas, the men on the *Sea Fever* wondered if they had made the right decision to stay with the boat through the night.

PART III

PART III

CHAPTER 18

Alone in the Night

ERNIE HAZARD NEVER NOTICED THAT THE WINDS had diminished slightly because the waves seemed just as enormous and their sound was still deafening. Most of the six-story waves continued to break on the raft's canopy, nearly crushing Ernie beneath their weight. Each time one struck, he had to quickly push the canopy back up to get the water off him. Between waves his bearded chin often fell upon his breast in utter exhaustion, but rest was impossible. The robotic exertion it took to balance the tiny capsule went on and on.

But he still had his fight. At one point, out of pure frustration, he angrily screamed a challenge at the seas: "Is that the best you got?"

Nightfall was closing in on Ernie's violent and desolate world. He had been battling for survival within the raft for five straight hours, all the while hoping for the long shot that another fishing boat might spot him. He now understood that for another boat to have any chance at finding him, he would have to first hear or see the boat approaching and then fire off a flare. Rather than dwell on the fact that he could barely hear above the waves, he told himself that should he spot a boat, or even a plane, his flare might be seen.

As the waves continued to thrash the raft, Ernie could tell that it had lost some air, but the sea was too frenzied for him to pull the pump from the survival bag and use it. He refused to worry about the raft's structural integrity in the face of the onslaught because nothing could be done. He simply hoped the raft's designers had pictured sixty- and seventy-foot waves when they chose the fabric and the sealant used to separate the air chambers. It was a good thing he didn't know that these same waves were cracking the oak ribs on the *Sea Fever* just a few miles away.

By 6 p.m. darkness had enveloped Ernie. The raft came equipped with a small red beacon on top of the canopy, but it had been ripped away in the first few minutes after the *Fair Wind* pitchpoled. It was as if he had lost his sense of sight. He forced himself to stay fully alert, for if the raft capsized now, he might not be able to maintain his grip on it. Should he become separated from the raft he would surely die. He refused to waver from the mind-set he had adopted in the first hour of the ordeal—I may die, but not without a fight.

Around 7 p.m. Ernie's worst fear came true: a snarling wave flipped the raft completely upside down and the vessel did not continue its roll. For a split second Ernie's feet were pointed toward the surface and his head was underwater as the seas came flooding into the overturned raft, smothering him. He thrashed and kicked to find the opening, but in the darkness the task was tougher and more disorienting than it had been earlier. Precious seconds ticked by as he held his breath and swung his hands along the raft's wall to find the door. He could sense the water seething around him, holding the raft down the way a cat pounces on a mouse. But then he was suddenly free. As he came up for air, the razor-sharp wind screamed around him, and immediately he felt its chilling bite. Groping and flailing wildly in the darkness, his hands at first felt nothing but foam and water. Finally, his fingers hit the raft and found the outside line that encircled it, which he clamped on to with a ferocious grip. He could not, would not, lose the raft.

Water cascaded from the ballast bag, which was now just above the ocean's surface. For a second Ernie thought about climbing atop the raft and trying to right it himself, but he quickly dismissed the idea and instead struggled to get inside the ballast bag and out of the wind. Now, on top of the upside-down raft and inside the ballast bag, he collapsed, panting and shaking from the effort and the cold. He kept his head at the opening of the ballast bag and gulped in big breaths of air and its precious oxygen. Then a terrifying thought sent an electric jolt through him: had the survival bag gotten washed out of the raft? In it were the flares and the water he'd need to survive.

Rain pelted the ballast bag in violent torrents, and the waves battered Ernie with such ferocity he was afraid they'd crack his back like a dried twig. Then he felt a wave slam the raft with such power it seemed like he was being propelled over a waterfall. He found himself, once more, completely submerged in the swirling water, gagging as he choked on the seawater that had caught him by surprise. He squirmed out of the bag and kicked toward the surface. Between the water and the air was a layer of foam, and he struggled, gasping, to get his head above the spume, which had the consistency of shaving cream. He swung his arms toward where he thought the raft would be, and as before, luck was with him. His hand hit the line. He grabbed it with cold fingers and slowly turned the raft until he could feel the edge of the doorway and the two-step plastic ladder, knowing that now the raft was right side up. Aided by a kicking motion, he first thrust his torso inside and then used his legs on the ladder to get the rest of his body in. More than a foot of water was sloshing on the raft's floor, and Ernie collapsed into it, trying to find the strength to get back into the sitting position opposite the door before the next wall of water descended.

His eyes stung from the salt and he groped about the raft until he felt the survival bag, relieved it was still safely tucked inside the raft. His heart was pounding so hard it felt like it would burst from his chest, but he used what little strength he had left to pull himself up and sit with his back against the canopy wall, already tensing again as he heard the next breaker roar down on him. This one broke after sliding beneath the raft, and Ernie felt his rubberized capsule sail down into the trough.

Ernie's mind begged for rest, for just a snatch of sleep, but letting his guard down for even a minute could end in disaster. He had to balance the raft to keep the door in the lee of the storm, or the sea would come flooding in and bury both him and the raft. The waves were not uniform in height, which made Ernie's situation all the more challenging. Twenty waves would hit the raft in the exact same way with the exact same power, and then suddenly one would be a bit larger, a bit steeper, and break directly on him.

The battle raged on with no letup for five more agonizing hours, and Ernie made it to midnight without mishap. He was halfway to dawn, halfway to what he hoped would be salvation. But the storm was not through. Sometime in the latter half of the night a breaker careened into the raft and he felt himself being lifted. The wave sent the raft over on its side and Ernie held position as best he could as he spun and tumbled in the dark void. Luckily, the raft did a complete 360-degree turn, and somehow Ernie maintained his sitting position. How many more hits could he and the raft take before one or the other came unglued?

Over and over he told himself, Ride it out, just ride it out. It's almost over. The most difficult part, though, was that he had no idea how long he would have to keep fighting. There was no finish line in sight. If he had a watch he could read in the dark, he could have marked off each hour, knowing he was getting closer to the storm's end, but without a watch, it was difficult to judge how much time remained until dawn. Nearly twenty-four hours after the freak storm began, the waves showed no signs of letting up. Just get through this night, thought Ernie. I can take this. Just a little longer.

CHAPTER 19

Dawn

Eastward, a hint of pale gray light faintly illuminated the desolate horizon of endless ocean. It was one of the most welcome sights Ernie Hazard had ever seen. He let out a long sigh. *Maybe today.*

He had made it through eleven punishing hours of complete darkness. Battered and bruised, he had managed to stay inside the raft all night by constantly balancing and maintaining his sitting position while fighting off overwhelming fatigue. Now he poked his head outside the raft's canopy and looked upon a monotonous landscape of towering gray-green hills of water streaked with white, as far as the eye could see. Fortunately, the waves had diminished in size, and the wind had calmed somewhat. The waves still had enough kick to knock the raft around, but they no longer broke under their own weight. Ernie, however, was still wary; he had come too far to let a wave sucker-punch him.

The skin on his elbows and back was raw and red from chafing against the raft's fabric, and his head, neck, and back ached. His body desperately craved sleep but all he could manage was a few seconds of fitful dozing before the motion of the seas again jolted him awake. Here was a new kind of torture, different from the life-or-death struggles of fighting to stay inside the raft. This was more insidious; each time he began to relax, the sudden motion of a wave jolted him from rest like a sadistic taskmaster poking him with a stick.

Ernie's ordeal was becoming as much a psychological battle as it was a physical one, but he held fast to the mind-set of a survivor rather than a victim. Ernie still believed that if he was to survive, he would need to do everything he could to increase his chances of being found alive. He did not pray because he felt his best chance was to fight. He needed to keep his mind sharp and his eyes vigilant. If he made it out of this hell alive, there would be plenty of opportunity to give prayers of thanks. Right now he knew he was on his own, and only *action* was going to see him through.

Under the circumstances, Ernie's clarity of thought and his refusal to be lulled into a false sense of security were triumphs in themselves. He knew there was no guarantee that he would ever be found. The hours of struggle could all be for naught because he simply did not know what the day would bring. He had hopes, but he kept them guarded. He wasn't even sure anyone knew the *Fair Wind* had gone down. Certainly no one on land would become concerned until the boat was overdue, on Wednesday, a full four days away. He also realized that the *Fair Wind*'s EPIRB had probably never gone off or he would have heard or seen a Coast Guard plane or helicopter by now. No, his only chance of being missed would have to come from one of the other fishing boats, and Ernie hoped that the men on the *Sea Fever* or *Broadbill* had become alarmed by the length of time that had gone by without a radio message from the *Fair Wind*.

* * *

A few inches of cold water sloshed around the bottom of the raft, and Ernie had to expend valuable energy pushing it out the door with a small paddle. Despite the effort, he was glad for the chore—it gave him something to do and offered a brief diversion from the discomfort of the cold, which he felt down to his very core.

Now that there was a bit of light illuminating the inside of the raft, he decided to open the survival bag and extract a can of water. He had been incredibly fortunate that he'd successfully endured the night without getting seasick, which would have increased the likelihood of weakness and dehydration. Still, his thirst was great as he held a ten-ounce can of water in his shaking hand. The can did not have a flip top and Ernie rummaged through the survival bag looking for a can opener, but all he found was a knife. The knife, however, had a blunt end rather than a point and was useless when it came to puncturing the can. Ernie saw the irony—the blunt-nosed knife was probably selected so that it wouldn't inadvertently puncture the raft, but now left him without a tool to open the can. He brought the can to his mouth and tried to bite a hole in the top, first with his front teeth, then with his incisors. The can was too thick.

Frustrated, he turned back to the bag and began looking through it again, careful not to remove its contents for fear a wave would slam the raft and wash everything out. Then he saw the can opener wedged at the bottom of the bag. He quickly opened the can and greedily drank down every drop. Almost immediately he felt revived. This was his first drink of fresh water in eighteen hours, and after all the salt water he had swallowed, it tasted fantastic. There were five cans left, and he decided not to drink again until the end of the day.

Also in the bag was a can of protein cookies, and Ernie ate one, savoring each small bite. He had not eaten since Friday, and he was ravenous from expending so much energy, but like the cans of water, he didn't dare consume any more cookies. With great willpower he closed the cookie tin and placed it back in the bag. He then inspected the bellows pump for the raft's air chambers and the signal flares inside the survival bag. There were two types of flares, several small hand-held flares and a canister of cartridges. Each cartridge was slightly larger than a pencil and was equipped with a firing pin. A six-pack of flares was in the canister and each one could be screwed onto the top of the cartridge. The instructions inside the survival bag explained that the cartridge could be fired and the flare would make an arc of light approximately one hundred feet long.

The survival bag really did mean survival to Ernie. Having fresh water eliminated the overwhelming temptation some castaways have to drink seawater, which, instead of relieving thirst, increases it as well as the corresponding dehydration. Castaways, even those who know the dangers of drinking seawater, often approach the act cautiously, telling themselves they will just take a few drops and rinse out their mouths, but they inevitably swallow a bit. Then they do it again, thinking that so little an amount cannot cause any harm, when in fact it will surely kill them.

The heavy sodium content of seawater must be removed by urinating, which, in the case of an already dehydrated person, triggers the body to use up precious bodily fluids from muscles, organs, and tissue in its effort to rid itself of sodium. It also causes brain damage by pulling moisture out of the brain cells, and delirium can set in within two hours of the initial consumption. Those who drink enough seawater hallucinate and sometimes climb out of a raft and enter the water, thinking they are stepping onto land or toward a familiar object. A particular chilling account was chronicled in the book *Albatross*, by Deborah Scaling Kiley and Meg Noonan. After abandoning the yacht *Trashman*, one of the shipwrecked men on the raft had consumed seawater and suddenly announced he was "going to get the car."

Sharks had been circling for hours, but it didn't stop him from leaving the raft and swimming toward what he thought was his car. His fellow castaways saw his head bob up on a swell and then heard a terrible scream before he was pulled under the waves by the sharks.

As grateful as Ernie was for the contents of his survival bag, he would have benefited from a more comprehensive one that contained a blanket in a waterproof bag, a first-aid kit with painkillers, a bailer, and a sea anchor. A sea anchor, also known as a drift anchor or drogue, is a device usually made of fabric, often funnel-shaped. The sea anchor is tethered to the vessel, and as the sea passes through it or is impeded by it, the drift rate of the vessel is slowed. This would have helped Ernie by keeping him closer to the last known position of the *Fair Wind,* increasing his chances of being found if a search was conducted. Ernie estimated that the winds and seas were pushing the raft to the southeast and if that drift continued he'd soon be off Georges Bank and away from any fishing boats. Sarcastically, he thought, Next stop, Spain. Rescue, if it were indeed coming, had to arrive soon.

As he drifted, Ernie thought back on the accident, wondering if there was anything Billy and he could have done differently. They had routinely monitored the weather forecasts before the storm caught them by surprise, and once in its grip, they had flooded the center lobster tank for stability, secured all the gear, and turned their bow into the growing waves. No, they had taken the right precautions and had done their best.

Thinking of the actions he and Billy had taken made him mourn for his lost crewmates, and those thoughts, more than the physical punishment he was taking from the ocean, caused the first crack in Ernie's determined resolve. He thought of Dave Berry, who never even had a chance, trapped down below in the bunk-room when the *Fair Wind* pitch-poled. Dave had been a pleasure to work with. Growing up in Marblehead, he had always loved the sea, and on these trips he kept a detailed log of where and at what depth they caught lobsters during different times of the year. Both Dave and Rob Thayer were young, twenty and twenty-two respectively, and Ernie felt close to them.

Billy, at age thirty-two, was almost the same age as Ernie. The two men had formed a close friendship, and Billy made it a point to introduce Ernie to all the important people in his life. Together they made an interesting duo. Billy was short and wiry while Ernie was tall and brawny, and both had thick beards, Billy's red-dish brown and Ernie's jet black. No one would mistake them for brothers but they looked out for each other as brothers do. Ernie had known Billy would be named captain of the bigger boat Charlie Raymond was building and Ernie had looked forward to being teamed with Billy on the new vessel.

How different it would be, thought Ernie, if his friends had escaped the *Fair Wind* and were here in the raft with him. Some-one to talk to, to bolster his spirits, maybe even to joke with to relieve the tension. Sure, they would have been packed tight, their elbows, knees, and feet hitting one another, but that little bit of discomfort would have been nothing compared to the peace of mind of having the whole crew in the battle together. Instead the men's lifeless bodies were likely trapped inside the *Fair Wind* lying on the bottom of the ocean.

The thoughts about his friends sent a deep despondency through Ernie, and he knew that for now, he had to force them from his mind. To do that, he kept as busy as possible. The ribbed air chambers that held up the raft's canopy were sagging from the pounding of the seas and appeared to have lost a significant amount of air. Ernie carefully attached the bellows hand pump to a valve and pumped air into the ribbed chambers. When he removed the pump, however, an ominous hissing sound came from the valve. Air was leaking from the valve itself. Ernie's mind raced, trying to think of a way to stop it. Using the knife, he cut a patch from the survival bag and then tied the patch over the valve with line from the raft's tether. His patch seemed to stem the flow of air, but not entirely. Over the next few minutes the canopy slowly deflated to the point where it was resting on his head, and so he took out the pump and once again sent air into the ribs and tied the valve off with the patch.

He tried to doze off, thinking that if he was not rescued today, he might have to stay awake all night because his chances of being found might be better in the dark when one of his flares could be seen. The constant advance of waves would not let him sleep, but he did shut his eyes and tried to conserve energy until a new hissing sound roused him into action. A valve on one of the main circular rings that kept the raft afloat was leaking, and Ernie scrambled to cut another patch from his survival bag. After the patch was ready he first used the pump to add more air into the chamber and then tied the patch over the valve.

As the morning progressed, Ernie fell into a routine of pumping both the arches and the circular ring every twenty or thirty minutes. He wasn't sure his efforts were making much of a difference but it gave him something to do. Survival experts know that keeping oneself productively occupied is crucial to maintaining the mental toughness to fight on rather than give up, and Ernie instinctively knew this. He also acknowledged that the leaks were replacing the waves as his main adversary and source of concern, and he wondered if there were leaks he couldn't see on the outside of the raft. No raft on the market could have survived unscathed the constant pounding of such giant seas, and Ernie also realized that his decision to keep the raft tethered to the *Fair Wind* for almost an hour had certainly strained the raft further. He was prepared, however, to live with that decision, and if he had to do it all over again, he'd make the same choice: to stay by the boat for as long as there remained an ounce of hope that its crew could escape.

The nearly constant pumping gave Ernie a brief diversion from the bone-chilling cold, but all he had to do was glance at his feet to know that hypothermia was taking its toll. They were numb and they had turned an ugly shade of purple. He tried massaging them, but it did little good. Periodically he peered out of the door, still hoping to see a boat, knowing time was running out.

CHAPTER 20

The Families Wait
for News

RNIE WAS NOT THE ONLY ONE WHO HAD JUST EXPE-
rienced the longest night of his life in this storm. Peter,
Sarge, and Brad had remained aboard the *Sea Fever*
crouched on the port side of the deck, feet braced against
the engine block, wondering if the next wave would end it all.
The pump dropped by the Coast Guard pilots had helped to stem
the flooding, but the waves still lifted the port side to precarious
heights, and each time the men looked down into the void on
the starboard side, they were reminded of how little separated
them from the cold and hungry sea.

For Brad, the hockey player, the pounding felt like being
checked into the boards from behind again and again. For Peter,
who had weathered plenty of storms with his father, the intensity of this one defied description. Sarge figured the experience
was not unlike being caught in a nighttime ambush, with no
retreat route. The cumulative effects of each hour of terror and

uncertainty were wearing down the men's fortitude, and it was a struggle to keep their primal fear at bay. They still needed to function, and might be forced to spring into action to save themselves with only a second to spare.

And so their goal throughout the night was simple: just hang on until morning. Each, however, had his doubts. At times they couldn't help but second-guess their decision not to be airlifted off the foundering boat by the helicopter, knowing that if something happened at night and they ended up in the water, Grant Moore on the *Broadbill* probably would not be able to save them. Their survival suits would keep them afloat and protected from hypothermia, but in the crazed, windswept, foam-filled seas they likely would not be found. The mental strain gnawed at all of them. How much more, they wondered, would the *Sea Fever* be able to handle before its wooden hull opened up and water came gushing in? It was probably best that they were unaware of what happened on the fishing vessel *Determined* just the day before. That was the vessel whose crew thought they could manage with a pump sent over from the cutter *Active,* and passed on the option of leaving their vessel for the safety of the cutter. Just an hour later the wooden planks on the *Determined*'s hull popped loose and the vessel began going down.

In the darkness the three remaining crew of the *Sea Fever* talked little, but they were all thinking similar thoughts. "I thought of Gary over and over," says Peter. "And I thought of his wife, remembering that she was pregnant with her first child. How could I ever tell her what happened? Those hours were so long and miserable I wondered if morning would ever come." Brad was in a similar state of despair: "I was absolutely crushed thinking about Gary. I'd worked side by side with him all summer, and I couldn't bear the thought that he was gone for good." Sarge couldn't help thinking how surreal it all felt. Just a few hours earlier he had been asleep in his bunk heading out for another routine trip, and now he was mourning his friend Gary. He remembered throwing the line so that it landed right next to Gary in the water, but Gary was so stunned he didn't move. They had done everything they could to save him and none of it worked.

Grant Moore on the *Broadbill* called Peter every half hour to check on the men and offer what little encouragement he could, and at 11 p.m. Grant's vessel was joined by a 90-foot swordfishing boat that also stood by in case they were needed. Twenty miles to the east, aboard the *Sea Star*, Bob Brown, Mike Sosnowski, and crew were now banging their way through torrential rain and house-sized waves toward Peter. The vessel's engine was under tremendous strain. Each time they reached the crest of a wave, the props came out of the sea, and when they plunged back into the water, the suddenness taxed the engine. Fortunately, the *Sea Star* was larger than the *Sea Fever*, and Bob Brown had more than twenty years' experience riding through storms, although he would later say, "I've never seen anything like that storm, and we've been through plenty of seventy- to eighty-mile-per-hour gales."

Knowing that both the *Broadbill* and the swordfishing boat were lying alongside Peter that night, Bob decided to veer a bit to the southwest to check on another 50-foot boat, the *Fair Wind*. He was not overly concerned that he hadn't heard from the boat, but figured he'd take a quick look, later saying, "It was still pretty nasty but when we got into the vicinity of the *Fair Wind*—where we thought her last position was—we looked for any lights, any sign of them. There was no sign but there was still an awfully big sea going and you could be in the trough when they could be up and vice versa, so it wouldn't be unusual that you didn't see them, but we tried."

Mike Sosnowski remembers that he and Bob took shifts on the wheel. "The seas were so bad that even if we went through a debris field we wouldn't have seen anything." Neither Mike nor Bob had any specific information about the *Fair Wind,* but in a storm like this one, every boat was vulnerable.

It was now early morning on Sunday, November 23, and using the radio—both the VHF and single sideband—they tried to raise the *Fair Wind,* without success. They knew it wouldn't be too unusual for a boat to lose its antenna, or for the sideband radio to lack the power to travel any great distance through the chaotic atmosphere. They hoped they'd find that the *Fair Wind* had gone to the aid of the *Sea Fever.*

Back on board the *Sea Fever,* Peter kept a grim vigil, monitoring the pump, checking in with Grant, and fighting overwhelming exhaustion. It wasn't until just before dawn that he and his crew felt the waves had lost enough power to allow them to rise from their wedged position without being knocked overboard. They also knew the cutter *Active* was on its way out to them, and for the first time in sixteen hours Peter, Brad, and Sarge allowed themselves to let their guard down just a bit. If the boat held together until dawn, just an hour away, they knew they would live.

On shore in Massachusetts, word of the ocean storm had spread beyond the Coast Guard as early as Saturday night. TV and radio reports described how the Coast Guard had responded to multiple boats in distress due to the surprise storm, but the first person outside the Coast Guard to learn that the storm's reach extended to Georges Bank was Linda Brown, Bob's wife and Peter's mother. The Coast Guard called her and told her that a man on the *Sea Fever* had gone overboard, but they did not know who it was. They also informed her that a helicopter had dropped a pump to the boat and the cutter *Active* was on its way to the crippled vessel. Linda, deeply pained, and not knowing if her own son was dead or alive, felt it was her duty to call the other family members, starting with Brad Bowen's parents.

"Brad's mother and I first found out about the accident when Linda Brown called us," says Brad's father, Tad. "She told us there had been a storm and that one of the crewmembers of the *Sea Fever* was lost overboard, but she didn't know who it was. I remember she was very kind and very worried. She gave us the number of the Coast Guard and said we should call them. We called the Coast Guard immediately and then we called them every hour for updates. The Coast Guard was fantastic. They told us everything they knew and were very patient with us. I remember we didn't sleep a bit that night, not knowing if Brad was alive or dead."

The Bowens felt they should call Brad's girlfriend, Suzanne, but decided not to cause her extra worry by mentioning that one of the men was missing. "When they called me," says Suzanne, "I was working at the Market Basket in Danvers. They didn't give me any details except to tell me there was a terrible storm offshore and a number of boats were in trouble." Suzanne left work and went home, immediately turning on the TV, which reported that a surprise storm had caused havoc to a number of boats off the New England coast. "I was really worried," says Suzanne. "Brad had already told me about going overboard on three different occasions, and I also knew that Bob Brown really pushed his men and that they worked through very nasty weather. I knew Brad was with Peter, and not Bob, but at that time I didn't know how careful Peter was and just assumed he was like his father."

Later, on Saturday night or early Sunday morning, the Coast Guard learned that it was Gary Brown who had been swept overboard, and decided that Gary's wife, Honour, should be contacted immediately and in person. The Coast Guard called the police department in Plymouth, the town where Gary and Honour lived, and explained the situation. They asked the police there to break the news to Gary's wife. Plymouth police were able to reach Honour by phone at home and told her they wanted to come over to see her and talk about Gary. Honour said, "What do you mean you want to come over and talk to me about Gary?"

"Well," said the police officer, "we can't talk about this over the phone. We just want to come over and talk to you about your husband."

Honour's first thought was that this was a crank call. She asked for the police department's phone number and called back. When she reached the same police officer, she knew it was no crank call. The police still wouldn't explain, and told her they would be at her house in a few minutes. Honour then called Gary's mother and told her about the call. His mother then called the police, and this time they explained what had happened. Gary's mother, in shock, decided not to tell Honour over the phone, but instead she, along with her other son, went straight to Honour's house, and they were there when the police arrived to tell Honour the terrible news.

Grant Moore had been so busy positioning his boat next to Peter's that he hadn't had time to think about the *Fair Wind*. But early Sunday morning he realized he had not heard from Captain Billy Garnos in quite a while. Grant repeatedly tried to raise Billy on the radio, and when no response came back, he grew alarmed and decided to call the *Fair Wind*'s owner, Charlie Raymond. "Using the sideband radio," recalls Grant, "I was patched through to Charlie and said, 'Charlie, we've been in a bad blow and I haven't heard from your boat. I think you better call the Coast Guard.'" (The Coast Guard does not start a search for an overdue vessel or one that is not communicating until the owner requests it.) Charlie immediately called the Coast Guard in Boston, and they in turn radioed the cutter *Active*, which was already steaming out to

Georges Bank, to inform them there might be a second boat in trouble. Charlie started calling the families of the men on his boat and explained the situation and that the Coast Guard had begun a search. Charlie was still hopeful, however. "At that point," recalls Charlie, "I was thinking maybe it was just a busted antenna, and everything would be OK."

CHAPTER 21

Heading Home and All Alone

TOMMY DUTTON HAD SEEN ALL KINDS OF SEA CON-
ditions while serving aboard the Coast Guard cutter
Active, but he recalled that the nighttime mission to assist
the *Sea Fever* was particularly harsh. "We got the shit kicked out
of us going out to the *Sea Fever,*" says Dutton. "It was awful—
big seas, very cold, and incredible winds. Although the *Active* was
210 feet, it was a lousy riding boat in bad weather. It had a lot of
free board and a high superstructure, and only drew six feet of
water forward and ten feet aft, so it really took some bad rolls."

The *Active* arrived at the *Sea Fever* on Sunday morning at
about 8 a.m. Seas had diminished to twenty to twenty-five feet
and a low leaden cloud cover added its gloom to the scene. Dutton knew that a man had been lost overboard from the crippled
vessel, and the 50-foot *Sea Fever* looked especially small, riding
up and over the soaring pewter-colored seas. When the lobster
boat was down in the troughs, the boat was completely hidden

by the waves, and only its rigging could be seen. The cutter made a wide circle around the *Sea Fever* to observe how the vessel was riding and to look at its damaged side.

Brad Bowen, exhausted and shaken, watched the cutter as if in a dream. "Seeing that cutter was one of the warmest things I ever experienced. We didn't really need them at that point, but it was still good to know they were on the scene . . . just in case."

Carl Helman, commander of the *Active,* raised Peter on the radio and asked if he and his crew wanted to be taken off the boat. Peter responded that the worst was over and that with the *Broadbill* standing by they should be OK. Helman then watched as the *Broadbill* maneuvered alongside the *Sea Fever* and handed over plywood, which Peter and his crew used to patch up the blown windshield. Peter also roped off the blown-out side of the pilothouse, then put the engine in gear to see how the boat responded. It seemed to ride well enough, and Peter informed the *Active* that his father, aboard the *Sea Star,* was due to arrive any minute and would escort him back to port. Peter also expressed his concern that no one had heard from the *Fair Wind,* and gave his best estimate of their last known position.

Coast Guard First District headquarters in Boston had also been in touch with Helman and explained that the owner of the *Fair Wind* had requested an immediate search. Helman then became the on-scene commander for the search and rescue of the missing vessel, which would give him control over both the cutters and the aircraft that would be involved in the search. Helman, realizing the *Sea Fever* was seaworthy, and had help standing by with more on the way, immediately headed the cutter toward the last known position of the *Fair Wind.* Joining the *Active* in the search for the *Fair Wind* was HU-16-E aircraft from Otis Air Force Base and a C-130 from Elizabeth City, North Carolina.

Active radioman Bill Gatter recalls discussing the *Fair Wind* with both Grant and Peter, trying to learn everything he could about the missing boat. "They told us the *Fair Wind* had an experienced captain and that the boat had all the latest equipment and survival gear. The problem was that no one knew exactly where the boat was at the time of their last communication. I didn't think there was a chance of finding anyone or even any debris if the boat had sunk because the search area was so large and the storm had been so powerful. We held out hope that maybe the fishing vessel had its antenna snapped off in the storm and couldn't communicate."

Not long after the *Active* plowed off to the southeast in search of the *Fair Wind,* Bob Brown and Mike Sosnowski on the *Sea Star* reached the spot where the *Sea Fever* and the *Broadbill* had been holding position. Peter and his father decided that Peter would immediately begin heading back to Hyannis, and that Bob would follow a mile behind him. Peter's radar and LORAN had been knocked out, so Bob would keep him on course.

Grant Moore on the *Broadbill* recalls talking to Bob when he arrived on scene. "Bob acted as if almost nothing had happened, and I couldn't believe how insensitive he was to what we had all been through. But that was Bob. I even think he insinuated that we should be working our gear!"

With Bob on the scene, Grant decided to conduct a search for the body of Gary Brown, but quickly realized how futile his efforts were in mile after mile of twenty-foot rollers. After searching for an hour he radioed Peter, and wished him a safe trip home. Grant then went back to his original location to retrieve his lobster gear. "We tried hauling gear late Sunday," says Grant, "but our hearts weren't in it, so we headed home."

As the damaged *Sea Fever* slowly headed west, Sarge, Brad, and Peter felt relief but no joy. "The mood," says Peter, "was sorrowful. There was no sense of happiness at being alive, just a hollow feeling about Gary. I kept going over what happened, wondering if we could have done anything different." In this exhausted and traumatized state of mind, the three remaining crew of the *Sea Fever* now faced an eighteen-hour trip back to Hyannis, Cape Cod.

The specifics of the *Sea Fever*'s ordeal hit the Massachusetts newspapers Sunday morning. The following brief article ran on the front page of the *Lynn Post:*

Winds Create Crisis at Sea, U.S. Coast Guard Rushing to Rescue

The U.S. Coast Guard embarked on several rescue missions late yesterday afternoon. One unidentified man was feared lost at sea as the Coast Guard vessel *Active* was rushing to the scene last night. The man was reportedly washed over in mountainous seas. Coast Guard spokesmen explained that a lobster boat, the *Sea Fever,* from an unknown port, with three people aboard, radioed a distress signal reporting the crewman overboard just before radio contact was lost. A fishing vessel, the *Broadbill,* was approximately two hours distant and was attempting to reach them.

The *New Bedford Standard Times* also ran a front-page story about the storm:

Stormy Seas Capsize Boats; Fisherman Lost

Violent seas hurled their fury at the fishing fleet yesterday, with a Plymouth man swept overboard and missing, the four-man crew of a sunken New Bedford vessel airlifted to safety, a New

Hampshire boat in port after a crippling at sea, and the Coast Guard said, two more city boats diverted for rescue efforts.

Plymouth lobsterman Gary Brown, who is in his 20's was swept overboard from the Hyannis-based *Sea Fever* and lost as the cabin of his boat was washed away 125 miles southeast of Nantucket.

The *Standard Times* article went on to chronicle the other boats in distress, including the *Barbara and Christine* and the *Christina*. There was no mention of the *Fair Wind*.

Although the newspapers had not yet learned that the *Fair Wind* had been out of contact since the height of the storm, roughly twelve hours earlier, family members of the crew had begun to hear that the boat was missing. Maria Pavlis, Billy's fiancée, received a call from Billy's mother Sunday morning. "She just said I needed to come over to the house," says Maria. "I thought maybe something happened to Billy, but because she was so calm, I didn't expect anything really bad. When I got there she told me that no one had been able to raise the *Fair Wind* on the radio and that Billy had not been heard from since Saturday morning. We didn't really know about the severity of the storm, so I was hoping that the boat just had trouble with its radio or maybe its engine was dead. I figured the Coast Guard would find them, or at least that's what I told myself and Billy's parents."

Dave Berry's mother, Nancy, first heard about the *Fair Wind* when her son Jeff called her and said the boat was missing. "There was nothing we could do but wait, and for me that meant pacing. The feeling of trepidation and dread was so overwhelming I just could not sit still, and I just kept walking back and forth through the house—anything to keep moving."

Dave's roommate, Jim Leboeuf Jr., first heard the news from Dave's father, who told him the *Fair Wind* had not been heard from in twenty-four hours and that the Coast Guard could find no trace of the boat. "I couldn't believe it," recalls Jim, "because we didn't even know about the storm. But I immediately knew things didn't look good if the Coast Guard, with all their aircraft and cutters, hadn't found the boat yet. I've fished Georges Bank myself and I knew you go out there at your own risk. And at the time we fishermen were playing Russian roulette in those fifty-foot boats. Both Dave and Billy were good friends of mine. I kept thinking how Billy almost lost his life on the *Horizon* a few years earlier when I was captain. We were hauling traps at Georges Bank at night and the seas were rough. I was in the pilothouse and heard a shout. I looked back toward the lighted stern and there was no one there. Then I saw a hand sticking up from the water about ten feet from the boat, and realized Billy had gone over. We were able to back the boat up and haul him in, and I said to him, 'You sure are lucky that I heard you. Had just another couple minutes gone by, we probably would have never found you in these seas and strong tides.' I couldn't help but think that Billy dodged that bullet, but this time the outcome looked different."

For other friends connected to the *Fair Wind,* reports in the Sunday paper about the surprise storm were what made them first suspect the *Fair Wind* might have gotten into trouble at Georges Bank. Fishing boat captain Hugh Bishop remembers that on Saturday in Marblehead there was no indication of how bad the seas were offshore. "The first time I even realized there was a problem," says Hugh, "was Sunday morning when I was reading the *Boston Globe,* and there was an article about how the Coast Guard had responded to a number of Maydays on Saturday, including one at Georges Bank. I called Bob Brown's wife, Linda, and she confirmed that the *Sea Fever* had been in trouble, but she didn't have all the details. And all she knew about the *Fair Wind* was that it hadn't been heard from in a while."

Hugh especially knew about the dangers of working offshore at Georges Bank, because he had fished the area in his 50-foot wooden boat for several years. "In 1979 I switched to working the waters closer to shore. I figured if I had nine lives, I'd used up eight of them, and I decided that I'd had enough close calls out at Georges Bank."

There was one person who would need Hugh's luck in the coming hours, and that was Ernie, alone and drifting eastward, headed off the Bank.

CHAPTER 22

Drifting East

SLATE GRAY CLOUDS SCUDDED OVER BLEAK ROLLING swells where Ernie's orange life raft continued to ride up, then down the twenty-foot rollers. Air continued to leak from the raft and Ernie had to pump more often to keep up with the increased outflow of air. It was now afternoon, and except for the gusting sound of the wind hitting the canopy, no noise broke the monotony. Ernie had been hoping to hear just one sound, the drone of a motor either from a plane or a fishing boat, but so far he seemed to be the only living thing left on the planet.

Beneath Ernie, however, were fish, from halibut to swordfish and the occasional shark, roaming the depths of the sea. Georges Bank, with its rich fisheries, hosted a wide array of sharks, but fortunately, by late November, the great white sharks would have moved south to warmer waters. However, blue sharks, which can grow to a length of nine feet and weigh four hundred pounds, stay out at the Bank as long as the water temperature stays above 50 degrees, which it was on this Sunday after the storm. With a

slender, sleek body, the blue shark is capable of quick accelera-
tion when it spots prey.

Life rafts have long been known to attract fish because they
represent something different to the fish: a floating object, shade
from the sun, a strange color, and perhaps the splashing noise of
a person bailing. Sharks come to check out the raft and then
might linger to feed on the nearby fish. The blue shark in particular may be attracted by the orange coloring of a raft; tournament
fishermen who go after this species know that orange is the blue's
favorite color, and so they use orange lures when angling. Ernie's
raft, like almost all life rafts, was a bright orange, designed to assist
searchers when scanning the seas. (The colors least appealing to
sharks are black or dark blue. Shark experts note that a shark is
more apt to attack the legs of someone in a bathing suit, where
skin is exposed, than someone in dark trousers or a wet suit.)

Blue sharks are opportunistic feeders and occasionally venture
into inshore waters, putting them in contact with people. Usually the sharks investigate swimmers and waders, and then glide
off, with the person never knowing that an eight- or nine-foot
predator has passed within a few feet. But every now and then, a
blue will act differently, and there have been attacks on humans.
This has happened along the eastern seaboard, including Cape
Cod, where an aggressive blue shark once ripped into a person
wading in Truro, resulting in a leg gash that required forty-six
stitches.

Another species of shark that prowls the waters of Georges
Bank in the fall is the mako, and this predator is even larger than
the blue—in fact, makos sometimes attack and eat blues. Makos
grow to twelve feet in length and 1,600 pounds, and are the
fastest of all sharks, capable of incredible bursts of speed that
enable them to capture and kill swordfish, tuna, porpoise, and just
about any other creature in the ocean. Like the blue shark, makos
have attacked humans. There have even been accounts of makos

that, after having broken free of a fisherman's line, turned back and attacked the boat. Makos are cousins to the great white shark, and one of the largest makos ever caught by man—weighing in at more than 1,500 pounds—was killed just thirteen miles off the Massachusetts coast.

Sometimes a shark, like a blue, will "set up shop" by a life raft, lurking just beneath it and using it as cover from which to ambush prey. The hanging ballast bag offers a temporary residence for smaller fish, which also attracts the attention of a shark. Often, sharks will bump and bang against the underside of a life raft, sometimes quite violently. The reason for this is not entirely clear, but it may be because the shark senses there is life—food—inside the raft.

Countless people who have survived in life rafts, such as author and castaway Deborah Scaling Kiley, have chronicled the terror they felt from sharks attracted to the raft. In her book *Albatross* she wrote, "Suddenly something slammed the *Zodiac*. I felt something under us, shimmering along the bottom. Another blow shoved us forward. We were being attacked by sharks . . . battered from all sides. They knew we were in here." Some of the survivors of the whaleship *Essex* faced an enormous shark as they drifted helplessly in their small whaleboat, prompting one of them to write that the shark was "swimming about us in a most ravenous manner, making attempts every now and then upon different parts of the boat, as if he would devour the very wood." Nathaniel Philbrick, author of the award-winning *In the Heart of the Sea,* explains that the shark circling the whaleboat was almost as large as the whale that sank the *Essex,* and that the shark actually tried to get its jaws around the small boat's sternpost in an effort to get at the men.

Ernie, ever pragmatic, did not concern himself with thoughts of sharks. He'd seen plenty of sharks on Georges Bank and knew a few still lingered on into the fall, but he had to deal with the more immediate threat of keeping air in his raft and keeping his mind functioning despite the cold. If a plane or a ship came by and he did not use the opportunity to fire off a flare, all his past effort might be wasted.

His limbs were stiff and sore, and although he changed positions frequently, he could not find a comfortable place to sit. He tried lying on his side but quickly abandoned that position, thinking the waves were still too big to risk being so vulnerable with no means of balancing if the raft took a particularly hard hit. Lying down also meant keeping more of his body in the water, because no matter how much he bailed, there was still water sloshing in the raft's bottom. Besides, there was really no time to lie down as air continued to leak out the raft's valves. Ernie wasn't sure if the problem was with the valve or maybe from his own improper resealing, since he had been unable to read the directions after they were swept out of the raft during the first hour of his ordeal.

Ernie may have cursed the sea but he never cursed the raft, certain that most other types of life rafts would never have kept him afloat for as long as the Givens model had. This was his life capsule and it had served him well in the face of terrific danger, and he attended to it carefully. Midafternoon he decided to repair the tattered nylon door, which had been ripped in three corners. Using the blunt-nose knife, he cut a section of a heaving line and proceeded to stitch as well as he could, knowing every little bit of protection from the wind was important.

Although stitching the door provided a minuscule measure of achievement, Ernie's continued action was indirectly fortifying his determination to fight on. Fixing things such as the door and putting patches over the valves was second nature to Ernie, as he had repaired motorcycles, cars, and even heavy equipment in the army. He had the mechanic's mind-set, quickly sizing up a problem and getting to work.

From past experience, he also knew about surviving close calls and the importance of luck. In fact, Ernie had been lucky in this sense all of his life. When he was ten years old, he was biking home from Lake Cochituate in Wayland, crossing the street, and didn't see the car speeding directly toward him. He was struck on the leg, then sent careening through the air. When he landed he was knocked unconscious and didn't come to until he was in an ambulance. Amazingly, he survived with nothing more than a broken leg and a few bruises and scrapes.

His string of close calls and good fortune continued. When he was twelve years old, on a cold winter's day on Dudley Pond, he was ice fishing alone when the ice gave way. The depth was over his head, and no matter how hard he tried to hoist himself out of the freezing water, he could not maintain a grip on the slippery ice. Luckily he wasn't too far from shore and was able to grab the tip of a tree branch, and slowly, hand over hand, secured a firm grip on the thicker part of the branch. Then he was able to hoist his torso up on the ice, followed by his legs. He then walked home.

But perhaps his closest brush with death happened when he was twenty-five and riding his motorcycle. A driver of an automobile ran a stop sign on a side road just as Ernie was cruising by on the main road. The front wheel of Ernie's motorcycle hit the side of the car. The impact stopped the motorcycle dead in its tracks, but the forward momentum sent Ernie flying up and over the car and dropped him in the center of the main road. Stunned, Ernie slowly got to his feet, amazed that he seemed to be in one piece with nothing broken. Had the car run the stop sign just a split second later than it did, Ernie would have been hit broadside and the outcome would have been very different.

And now, shaking with cold inside the raft, he knew he needed another stroke of luck or the raft would become his coffin. The afternoon was waning, and Ernie knew that the air temperature of about 45 degrees would drop during the night. He had now been either wet or in the water for more than twenty-four hours. His core temperature likely had dropped, perhaps to as low as 94 degrees, and the chill continued its inexorable march from his extremities toward his torso. With each passing hour his blood thickened and slowed while his capillaries constricted, causing his feet to become swollen, purple lumps. The cold had become a part of his very being, as if he'd never been warm, and he fantasized about a hot shower.

Adding to his discomfort, only a single layer of fabric separated him from the ocean, and the cold water beneath him was sucking away his body heat. (Today's rafts are outfitted with an air chamber on the floor for insulation against the sea, but back in 1980 most had only a bare uninsulated floor and many did not have the canopy that was saving Ernie's life.) He tried to keep his mind on his tasks of bailing and pumping but his thoughts kept returning to the fact that he had not heard a single search plane or helicopter the entire day. As the raft rode the waves to the east, Ernie thought, I'm heading in the wrong direction. If anyone is looking for me they better search this edge of the Bank. He tried to calculate how far he might have drifted from the *Fair Wind*'s last location, but when he considered the storm he had just endured, he estimated his drift to be between twenty and sixty miles. He had no real way of knowing if he was even still on Georges Bank.

Despite suffering from the cold and a terrible ache throughout most of his body, Ernie was in far better shape than most victims in similar situations because the extreme cold had not yet affected his judgment. Hypothermia quickly renders the thinking process disjointed and sluggish because the slow circulating blood doesn't bring the brain enough oxygen. Should Ernie have fallen into a state of confusion and indifference, he would likely not have continued his pumping schedule, and the raft might have completely collapsed.

* * *

The pale light coming through the clouds began diminishing as evening closed in on Ernie and the raft. A part of his brain relived the accident over and over, and Ernie battled to keep those thoughts from taking over. Keep busy, he told himself, just keep bailing and pumping, forget about what happened. His mood had been relatively steady up to this point, and he knew instinctively that should it start careening between highs and lows, he might not recover from one of the lows.

His mind struggled back and forth between dealing with what he could control and thinking about rescue, thinking about what-ifs. What if no one knows the boat sank? . . . What if I go another day, another two? Without having to fight the waves he had too much time to think, and a particularly terrible thought now bubbled up. Was the *Sea Fever* OK? It had been the closest boat to the *Fair Wind,* the one Billy had been talking with on the radio during the beginning of the storm. Theirs would be the first boat crew to wonder why they hadn't heard from the *Fair Wind.* But if the *Sea Fever* had gone down, said Ernie to himself, who knows when one of the other boats would miss the *Fair Wind*? He considered the scenario that the Coast Guard might, at this very moment, be searching for the *Sea Fever,* not even aware that his boat had sunk. If that was the case, he thought, everything depended on whether the *Fair Wind*'s EPIRB signal was activated and picked up.

He tried pushing these what-ifs out of his mind, but they kept coming. What if the *Sea Fever* crew are in a life raft just like me and time's running out for them . . . or what if they went down so quick they couldn't get out? The same monstrous wave that capsized our boat could have done the same to them. Ernie considered the bleak possibility that if the captains of the *Sea Fever* and the *Fair Wind* had spoken only to each other, and both boats were gone, no other vessel would miss either one immediately. He tried to recall if Bob Brown on the *Sea Star* had been working the Bank, but he just couldn't remember. He felt fairly certain that the *Broadbill* with Captain Grant Moore was out on the Bank before the storm, but he wasn't sure whether or not that boat had been heading back to port before the storm hit.

Ernie was starting to feel sorry for himself, and to change his focus he directed his thoughts away from rescuers and back to his raft. What do I have to do to survive another day, another two days, or more? he asked himself. I'm going to pull this off. I didn't spend all this time fighting just to give up now. Ernie simply refused to accept that everything he had done thus far would only lead to a slow death, a fate worse than the one suffered by his crewmates.

CHAPTER 23

The Search

PLOWING THROUGH TWENTY-FOOT SWELLS, THE COAST Guard cutter *Active* arrived at the *Fair Wind*'s last known position by midafternoon on Sunday. Tommy Dutton stood out on the deck with binoculars in hand and scanned the seas for colors and shapes other than the gray ocean. He was searching not only for the boat itself but for anything that might catch his eye: bait buckets, barrels, a life raft, an orange survival suit, a life jacket, or a body. But nothing interrupted the dark rollers. "I didn't have much hope of us finding anything," says Dutton, "particularly not someone alive, because I knew what the conditions were like the day before."

The *Active*'s radioman, Bill Gatter, and Quartermaster Second Class Wayne Hennessy agreed. "I didn't think there was a chance of us finding anyone or even any debris, because the search area was so large," says Gatter. Hennessy was hoping they'd get lucky and find the *Fair Wind* still afloat because "if it wasn't, we doubted anyone would be found alive in late November."

The Boston operations center gave the cutter a search area to concentrate on based on the estimated drift of the *Fair Wind* with winds and currents. "In addition," recalls Operations Officer Dave Nicholson, "we decided to drop our own data buoy to try and get another sense of the drift. Our data buoy indicated the search should extend a little farther to the east, so we started expanding our hunt beyond the initial area."

The overall search area, however, was enormous, covering five thousand square miles, and aircraft launched from both Cape Cod and Elizabeth City, North Carolina, probably had a better chance than the *Active* of spotting any sign of the *Fair Wind* or its crew. Helicopters could not be used because the search area was beyond their range. This search would be harder than looking for the proverbial needle in the haystack; it was like looking for a needle in an entire field of hay.

As evening approached, the men on board the *Active* were growing more disheartened about the chances that the *Fair Wind* was still afloat. They knew that the planes hadn't spotted so much as a life ring, and as dusk drew its curtain over the ocean, the Coast Guard men now felt they were no longer conducting a search and rescue mission, but merely a search. The crewmen were exhausted after weeks at sea and the events of the past two days, and some figured that since the current search was for a lost cause, they might as well steam back to land to be home in time for Thanksgiving. The *Fair Wind,* they thought, had sunk and disappeared forever.

Boats the size of the *Fair Wind* vanish all too often, never leaving a clue as to what went wrong, and never giving up their dead. Sometimes even large ships disappear without giving a Mayday, such as the *Grand Zenith* and the SS *Poet.* The *Grand Zenith* was a 642-foot Panamanian tanker making a voyage between Nova Scotia and Providence, Rhode Island, in December 1976. On board was a crew of thirty-eight. The ship disappeared somewhere northeast of Cape Cod and the crew were never seen again. Nine days of searching by the Coast Guard turned up a grand total of two life jackets from the ship and nothing else. In the case of the SS *Poet,* a 522-foot freighter that crossed the Atlantic just one month before the *Fair Wind* went down, not a single item was ever recovered from the missing ship after an exhaustive ten-day search. The *Poet* was a 13,500-ton converted World War II troop ship carrying grain, heading from Delaware to Gibraltar and then on to Egypt. Whatever happened to the ship must have been sudden and cataclysmic, because a distress call was never received by the Coast Guard or any other vessels.

In another twist of fate, the Coast Guard Board of Inquiry released its official statement that the *Poet* was a casualty of the sea on the same day the men on board the *Active* concluded that the *Fair Wind* was a goner.

When boats the size of the *Fair Wind* disappear without issuing a radio Mayday, the cause of the accident is never known. On-board fire, explosion, capsizing, blown hatch covers, smashed windshields, cracked hulls, or a myriad of other events can sink a boat, but when the crew doesn't even have time to radio a distress call, another incident should be investigated: collision. Large ships run over small boats probably much more often than Coast Guard statistics suggest, merely because the smaller boat often ends up on the bottom of the sea and there is no way for authorities ever to determine the exact cause of the disappearance. The larger vessel either never knows they hit the boat or they know exactly what happened but refuse to stop. Every now and then, however, a crewmember from the sinking vessel escapes and lives to tell what really happened. Such was the case after the sinking of a 92-foot trawler, the *Starbound,* returning from Georges Bank in August 2001.

Joe Marcantonio, the captain of the *Starbound,* had just ended his night watch in the bridge and, after turning the watch over to crewman James Sanfilippo, went below to get some sleep. Just before 1 a.m. Joe was awakened by Sanfilippo's shouts that they were going to be run down by a ship. Joe dashed to the pilothouse and couldn't believe his eyes. The steel bow of an enormous ship was just a few feet away. In the next second the ship slammed into the *Starbound*'s port bow with a terrific crash, followed by a sickening scraping sound as the ship's steel hull slid along the length of the fishing boat. The bow of the *Starbound* had received a mortal blow, and the vessel immediately started sinking bow first, while water roared into the pilothouse, which had lost part of its port side. Like Ernie, Joe briefly found himself trapped in the flooded pilothouse in total darkness. He was able to swim clear of the sinking boat, and hollered for Sanfilippo and two other crewmen, Mark Doughty and Thomas Fronteiro, who had been sleeping below. The float-free life raft had self-inflated, and Joe crawled inside, expecting to see his crew emerge from the sinking ship. Instead all he saw was the larger ship's stern fade into the night. He called for his crew again, but there was only silence as the *Starbound* was swallowed by the sea.

Joe was more than a hundred miles out at sea, in the dead of night, and he prayed that the EPIRB activated as it should have. All he could do was wait. Adding to the shock and grief of losing his crew were his thoughts of his father, Cosmos Marcantonio, who had been the skipper of the *Captain Cosmos,* an 86-foot trawler. Cosmos Marcantonio was only thirty-six years old in September of 1978 when he steamed out to Georges Bank, ran into a storm, and disappeared with his crew of five other fishermen. Joe thought to himself, So this is what it was like for you, Dad.

In the pitch-black raft Joe groped for the survival bag, and when he located and opened it, he extracted a flashlight, but even after turning it on, his vision was blurry from the diesel fuel that had gotten into his eyes. He located the flares but could not read the instructions. He was shivering uncontrollably, and with a shaking hand he held the flashlight on the instructions and then moved his head so his eyes were just inches away from the print, but still he could not read the words. The flares were similar to the ones in Ernie's raft, each a long thin tube, and Joe didn't know which end was the one where the flare fired out of. His frustration was mounting and he told himself, Take it slow, try a flare now so that when a plane comes the next will fire properly. Since he wasn't sure which end of the tube was up, he made sure he leaned way outside the raft before he released the firing mechanism. Then a quick hiss, and the flare shot directly down into the ocean. He'd wasted a precious flare, but at least now he knew how to hold it.

Three long hours went by with the raft drifting on black swells in a black night. Then Joe heard a jet approaching, and before he even had time to fire off a flare, the jet came roaring directly over his raft, just two hundred feet above the sea. The jet was a Falcon, and its pilots had first homed in on the EPIRB, and then spotted the small beacon on the top of Joe's raft. The jet banked hard and came back, and again flew directly over the raft so that Joe knew for sure he'd been seen. The pilots relayed the information of the raft's location to Coast Guard headquarters, who in turn sent a nearby lobster boat to pick Joe up. Joe was rescued from the sea at dawn, but not from his trauma. In the weeks that followed he suffered from post-traumatic stress disorder and unbearable grief.

The ship that sank the *Starbound* might have gotten away with murder were it not for the U.S. Coast Guard activating the Automated Mutual Assistance Vessel Rescue System the instant they picked up the EPIRB from the sinking vessel. The system identifies all ships registered in the program within two hundred miles of an activated EPIRB, so that they can assist with the search and rescue. It was through this system that the Coast Guard discovered that a 541-foot foreign tanker was the closest ship to the EPIRB signal. The Coast Guard tried to radio the tanker several times but got no response, and it wasn't until two days later when the tanker arrived in Newfoundland, Canada, that the Coast Guard's suspicions about the tanker were confirmed. A 100-foot-long scrape was found on the side of the tanker, bearing paint marks of the same teal color as the *Starbound*'s hull. Justice then ground to a snail's pace because the incident involved the treaties and admiralty laws of the United States and two foreign countries.

Legal wrangling and punishment, however, were the last thing on Joe Marcantonio's mind after the accident. Nothing could change the fact that his friends were gone, his boat was at the bottom of the sea, and life as Joe had known it before the accident was irrevocably altered.

Sunday night brought an eerie silence as the wind all but ceased, and Ernie Hazard strained to hear what he hoped would be the drone of an airplane engine coming out of the coal black sky. He was talking to himself, debating the merits of forcing himself to stay awake or trying to get some much-needed sleep. On the one hand, he wanted to be ready to fire off a flare should he hear or see a plane or a ship, but on the other hand, his unbearable weariness was making each minute feel like an hour. Sleep deprivation had replaced the pain and discomfort of the cold as his number one misery.

To keep his spirits and his strength up he had eaten another cookie and drunk another can of water just before the sun set. He had four cans of water and a few cookies left. Ernie had no idea how long he would need to make them last, but was determined to stretch them out as long as he could.

Now the darkness heightened his sense of loneliness and he craved the company of another human being, the sound of another voice. The feeling of isolation was intense, but for Ernie not as debilitating as it might have been for someone who had never truly spent time alone. Some people go through entire lives avoiding occasions where they are alone, but not Ernie, who had often enjoyed being alone and independent. Of all his life experiences, none prepared him for his current predicament better than his solitary bike ride from Washington to Mexico.

Ernie came up with the idea for the journey when he was twenty-five years old, and instead of just talking about it, he had the nerve to do it. He quit his job, bought a one-way ticket to Seattle, purchased a bicycle, and began heading south. When he began the trip he didn't really have a goal in mind, but thought it would be nice if he could keep riding until he reached Mexico. Very little planning went into the trip because he felt he could learn as he went along. He had only a few dollars in his pocket, and little more than some clothing, a tent, and a sleeping bag in his bike's saddlebags. Ernie never knew where he would spend the night, but somehow he always found a campground or met people who invited him to stay at their house or camp in their yard. The trip was an eye-opener for Ernie in that it helped forge his growing belief that he could adapt to most any situation, and do so with little help from others. He loved the fact that each day offered something new, something different. When problems occurred he tended to view them as minor challenges that came with the territory, and resolving those challenges added to his sense of well-being.

And so now, alone in the raft, he was not terrified by his aloneness and isolation. Still, he couldn't control all of his thoughts, and he remembered the dinner with his crewmates at the Backside Saloon. Was it really just four days ago? he wondered. It could have been a lifetime ago, and thinking of the dinner caused him anguish, knowing everything was gone: his three friends, the *Fair Wind,* and his prior life, which had seemed to be going so well. To push such thoughts away, he turned to the repetitive chores of bailing and pumping. The tasks not only kept him busy, but they were necessary, and the simple results of more air in the raft and less water in its bottom were positive outcomes, and that was exactly what his psyche needed.

Not once did Ernie try to ignore his situation or deny his new reality. He knew the odds were now against him, and he knew any number of events, from a major leak to a new storm, could end his life within hours. But when he started to dwell on such things, the steely voice inside him would speak up. Come on, Hazard, keep it going. Don't go soft now. Roll with the punches, keep doing what you're doing.

From the beginning he accepted what had happened. There is a fine line between acceptance and resignation. He simply kept an open mind, and was honest with himself that he had no idea of the final outcome, telling himself that he had done—and would continue to do—the things that would help his odds.

Still, no human can work and function without sleep, and he finally allowed himself to nap. The seas had dropped to fifteen feet, and the raft rode the long swells easily, without the pitching and plunging motion of that morning. His sleep was fitful, more an intermittent doze than the restorative deep sleep that his body so desperately needed. He would doze for thirty minutes at most, and that would only bring him through the first two of the five stages of normal sleep. The sleep deprivation wasn't just deplet- ing Ernie's energy; sooner or later it would slow his ability to react to change, make quick and logical decisions, and perform tasks. Even worse, one of the symptoms of prolonged sleep deprivation is hallucination, and Ernie could still end up like the castaway who drank seawater and then stepped out of the raft "to get the car."

CHAPTER 24

Almost Out of Time

AT THE COAST GUARD COMMAND CENTER IN BOSTON, Lieutenant Robert Eccles had not given up on finding the men of the *Fair Wind,* although he was convinced the storm had sunk the boat. He was exhausted, along with Chief Petty Officer James Fay, Lieutenant Joseph Duncan, and Lieutenant James Decker, from two days of coordinating search and rescue missions. Eccles usually felt great emotion when handling cases in which a mariner drowned, such as Gary Brown on the *Sea Fever,* but the level of activity at the command center that weekend was so high he simply didn't have time to become preoccupied with sadness and grief. "In the past," says Eccles, "when working with distress calls that ultimately ended with a loss of life, the personal trauma that I had to deal with surfaced much sooner because I had time on my hands. But not this time. The work we were performing was simply nonstop." Eccles and fellow staff members had decided that they needed additional assistance besides the two Coast Guard airplanes already searching Georges Bank. Eccles knew that if there were survivors in a life raft, they were near the end of what they could endure of the cold, if they hadn't expired already.

Lieutenant Duncan, using the hot-line phone in the command center, called the U.S. Naval Air Station in Brunswick, Maine, and explained the situation. It was agreed that at dawn on Monday morning, an enormous P-3 long-range patrol plane, with a crew of eleven, would set out for Georges Bank. Commander William Lash and Lieutenant Commander Alfred Linberger would be in charge of the search, and the plane could carry enough fuel to keep them aloft all day. The P-3 is a four-engine turbo-prop Orion aircraft built to detect submarines using electronic scanning equipment. The plane's reconnaissance capacity would be an advantage in searching for the *Fair Wind*, but because the plane was designed to locate submarines with electronics, it wasn't the best aircraft from which to visually look for a life raft. Unlike the Coast Guard HC-130, which has large windows for searches to scan the ocean below, the crew of the P-3 had limited visibility. Personnel manning the Boston Coast Guard command center knew this, but they had to use whatever resources they could, as time was running out for any survivors.

For Ernie, time stretched as endlessly as the ocean surrounding him. It was the hour just before dawn, the hour some say is the darkest of the night. Attaching the pump to the valves was difficult in the blackness, but Ernie had performed the task so many times he could do it by touch alone. Now, however, his frozen limbs felt sluggish, and for the first time his numbed hands gave him difficulty. His thickened blood labored to reach his extremities, and his task of pumping the raft took a bit longer each time he performed it.

His feet were now mere raw lumps of flesh, and Ernie tried to remember what it felt like to be warm, without the terrible aches. He rubbed and massaged his feet, but he wasn't sure if that was what a person should do for frostbite. He shook his head, tugged on his beard, and tried to recall the proper treatment for frozen limbs. The treatment, he told himself with a pained smile, is to get warm. The treatment is to get your ass out of this raft, get dry, and get off the ocean!

He couldn't see his feet in the dark, but he knew they were in bad shape. They were so waterlogged that when he rubbed them, it almost felt as if the skin would come off. He barely had any sensation at all from his ankles to his toes, and he wondered if he'd ever get it back, and if he'd ever be able to walk again. When the word *amputation* popped into his mind, he shook his head and, with a grunt, got to his knees and crawled toward the raft's opening. Sticking his head outside, he could not discern the skyline, but up above he saw a few stars in various patches. The cloud cover was breaking and the day ahead held the promise of sun. *I haven't seen the sun in . . . how long?* He thought back to the day before the accident, Friday, and remembered the sunset he watched from the pilothouse with Billy, Rob, and Dave. *How many days ago was that? What day is today?* It took him a minute to realize that it was Monday, and that the *Fair Wind* went down on Saturday, just two days ago. *Could it really have only been two days ago?* It seemed to Ernie that time had been altered in a strange way, that the period of suffering since the pitch-poling was as long as his entire life before the accident. And in some ways this period in the raft felt even longer, a nightmare without end. Time was starting to lose meaning, but he was too weary to care.

A common response to a disastrous accident is to relive the initial ordeal, and Ernie couldn't help but think back to Saturday morning and how he was asleep in his warm bunk without the slightest advance warning that a hurricane was about to assault the fishing grounds. He remembered it was about this same hour of day, just before dawn, that he climbed into the pilothouse and listened to Billy say it looked like a big blow was coming because it was getting worse by the minute. And he bitterly thought of the weather forecast he heard at that hour and how the seas were already double what the meteorologists predicted. It was as if the weather report was backward: instead of forecasting what might be expected, it was giving conditions that had occurred three hours earlier. Again, Ernie tried to turn his mind away from what went wrong—it was just too debilitating to think his friends had died because of a screwup in the weather forecast.

Fortunately, Ernie had not fallen into the trap of blaming himself for what happened, as many survivors unreasonably do. Throughout history, survivors of major catastrophes rack their minds and second-guess every little decision they made, thinking that if they had just done one thing differently, the whole accident could have been averted. Over and over they go through each second, each reaction, as the calamity occurred, and they begin to attribute outcomes to their own action or inaction. In hindsight they see how they might have made better decisions that might have averted the accident, but they don't cut themselves any slack by reminding themselves that hindsight is twenty-twenty. And so they reproach themselves, adding depression and guilt to the trauma they are already dealing with, and in some cases this is the tipping point in their struggle to endure, and they slip into apathy.

Of course, apathy could still arise within Ernie simply because the sea and the cold were wearing him down. Fatigue, hypothermia, sleep deprivation, and hunger were just some of the stresses grinding away at his physical and mental health. He had been looking at his situation logically and realistically, and he knew from the start, from the moment he forced himself to swim downward to get out of the flooded pilothouse, that he had been presented with a series of choices. Even now, with his mind growing listless, he knew the choice was still there: he could keep willing himself to endure more, or, just as easily, will himself to die as quickly as possible. And there was the third option, the easiest of all, which was to be indifferent to his fate.

The men who survived the sinking of the *Essex* by taking to the small whaleboats battled this kind of despair, and author Nathaniel Phlibrick, writing in *In the Heart of the Sea*, described how Owen Chase awoke one morning to find fellow castaway Isaac Cole despondent in the bilge of the boat. Chase later wrote, "All was dark in his [Cole's] mind, not a single ray of hope was left for him to dwell upon." Chase remembered Cole asserting that "it was folly and madness to be struggling against what appeared so palpably to be our fixed and settled destiny." The choice between fighting onward or giving up was similarly illustrated by the story of Howard Blackburn and Tom Welch, who became lost in their dory on a frigid January day in 1883 while fishing off Newfoundland. During their second night adrift, suffering from excruciating frostbite, each man made a decision about whether to fight on or give up. Welch turned to Blackburn and said, "Howard, what is the use, we can't live until morning, and might as well go first as last." Welch soon died, but Blackburn defied his prediction about living past morning, and he survived three more days before he was found and nursed back to health, minus several fingers lost to frostbite.

Ernie dozed for a few minutes, until his internal clock forced him awake to pump air into the raft again. He noticed that beyond the nylon canopy there was just enough gray light for him to look through a crack in the door and see the ocean sliding beneath the raft. It was clear which direction the sun would emerge from and that was the direction he was drifting, ever eastward, off the Bank. He stuck his head out the door. Gone were the sharp edges of the waves, replaced by smooth, gently rolling swells. Instead of mountainous, jagged peaks, these waves looked like rounded foothills, and the sea a monotonous undulating void. Ernie may not have known it, but sensory deprivation was conspiring with the cold to further wear him down. There was nothing to divert him from his misery and pain, not even a breath of wind to ruffle the ocean, and every ten-foot roller was the same as the next. Twenty-four hours earlier Ernie was in sensory overload, tumbling in mountainous waves and assaulted by shrieking winds, whereas now all was calmness and quiet.

Ernie was struck by his utter insignificance on this endless ocean plain, and he felt like an ant clinging to a scrap of vegetation, adrift on the indifferent sea. How would a search plane ever spot me? he wondered. Everything has to go my way: a plane must fly close enough that I can hear it and then I've got to fire off a flare within a second or two. He made sure the flares were easily accessible inside the survival bag, and he kept the bag unzipped. Should a plane pass overhead while Ernie was dozing or if he didn't fire off a flare in time, the plane would continue on and maybe never cover this part of the search grid again. And if Ernie drifted off the Bank and had the incredible long-shot odds of being in the path of a freighter or tanker, chances were the ship's crew would never notice him. In fact, he had better odds of being run down by a ship than being seen by one, since so many ships no longer post a lookout but instead rely entirely on radar and a collision alarm to alert them to other vessels. Many castaways who have survived long ordeals on the open sea report that ships passed within less than a hundred feet and never stopped, despite the screams of the castaways and even the shooting off of flares. The castaway looks at the huge deck gliding by, hoping to see another human standing there, but instead it's as if no one is aboard the ship and it's being controlled remotely from a thousand miles away. The castaway's frustration and bitterness at intersecting the path of a ship—in thousands of miles of empty

ocean—and still not being seen is sometimes more than he can
bear.

Ernie wondered when the sun would be strong enough to break
through the low thin clouds, and he hoped that its rays would
provide a bit of warmth inside his domed raft, which felt more
and more like a stainless-steel walk-in refrigerator. Next, his mind
wandered to creature comforts, imagining the taste of hot coffee
and the way it would spread its heat into his stomach and drive
out the cold. He pictured lying down in a dry bed, with layers
and layers of blankets surrounding him. And when he thought
of his mother and brothers, it all became too much, and he
turned his attention back to pumping air into the raft.

When the pumping was finished he looked outside again. A
weak bit of sunlight filtered through the cloud cover to the east.
And then he spotted the first form of life he'd seen since his
ordeal began. A shearwater, a pelagic bird that spends almost its
entire life at sea, flew by the raft. The bird flew from west to east,
the same direction Ernie was drifting. Through the years, Ernie
had seen plenty of shearwaters and other pelagic birds out at
Georges Bank, and he knew many of these birds had never even
seen a human, a boat, or anything man-made. He hoped this bird
would be different, that it would see not just a life raft, but a
Coast Guard cutter. He knew time was running out.

CHAPTER 25

At the Edge of
the Bank

A S THE *SEA FEVER* APPROACHED THE DOCK IN HYANNIS,
all Peter could think of was getting off the boat. The
meticulously maintained vessel that had set out to sea
just four days earlier was now a mess, with debris strewn about
below, water still sloshing in the bilge, and the shattered starboard
side of the pilothouse a sorrowful reminder of where Gary had
been hurled from the boat. For the past eighteen hours Peter
had been thinking of Gary, picturing the barrel-chested, red-
headed Irishman on the wheel during the storm, his left hand
with a white-knuckle grip on the wheel and his right hand on
the throttle. Then the wave hit, the boat tipped 90 degrees, and
Gary was swept away. But Peter had one last look at Gary, when
he was behind the boat, faceup in the water with a glassy-eyed
stare, looking at nothing. Yes, Peter, the distraught twenty-two-
year-old captain, wanted to run from this death trap of a boat as
soon as it touched the dock.

Peter knew, however, that leaving the boat immediately might not be an option, because his father was right behind him in the *Sea Star* and might insist they clean up the mess below. Surprisingly, though, when they got the boat tied up, Bob let them leave. Peter embraced his wife and Brad his parents. Neither man said much, totally overcome by the reunion with loved ones. "To this day," says Brad, "it's still too overwhelming to describe what it was like to see my parents standing there."

Brad's father, Tad, remembers that once the Coast Guard had informed him that his son was alive, back on Sunday, he kept in contact with Bob's wife, Linda, to find out when the *Sea Fever* would be arriving in port. "My wife and I packed the car with lots of food and went down to Hyannis and waited. When the boat came in there were hugs and tears, but Brad didn't say much about what happened out there. He and his crewmates looked pale, drawn, and exhausted." When Brad finally made it home, he found it difficult to talk about what happened, and neither his girlfriend, Suzanne, nor his parents pressed him. "The only thing I remember Brad saying," recalls his father, "was that the storm came out of nowhere, and he kept wondering how the weather service could have missed the forecast so badly."

Sarge had no one waiting for him; he had specifically asked the Coast Guard not to call his mother, because she was ill from cancer. Instead he talked to the crew on the *Sea Star* and to Frank Collins, who owned a wholesale lobster company and always met the Brown boats when they came back from the fishing grounds to buy the lobsters. Earlier Frank had received a radio message from Bob Brown, who told him when they would arrive as well as what happened to the *Sea Fever* and how nobody had heard from the *Fair Wind*. "Bob made it clear," says Frank, "that he wanted things low-key, and to make sure there was no press at the dock." Frank didn't tell anyone about what had happened, because he did not want the media swarming the shell-shocked crew of the *Sea Fever*. If word got out, TV reporters would be lying in wait, hoping to get the tears on film.

Frank remembers he took one look at Peter getting off the boat and could tell what an awful toll the accident had taken. "He looked like he'd been hit with a baseball bat, almost in shock. He was a good captain and losing a man was really hard on him. Bob, on the other hand, was unemotional. He never let his feelings show. He was thinking more about how he had to get the *Sea Fever* repaired than about what happened."

And the *Sea Fever* would need extensive repairs. Besides the damage to the wheelhouse and the interior of the boat, the wooden hull had twelve cracked ribs. "When I found out how many ribs were cracked," says Sarge, "I really thought it was a miracle that the boat had stayed afloat for as long as it did." Sarge looked at the *Sea Fever*, now tied to the dock, and it was as if he saw the boat for the first time, recognizing just how small it was for the size of the seas they battled. With the front windows boarded up and the starboard side of the pilothouse house roped off, the boat appeared vulnerable and fragile.

Sarge remembered his "storm promise" to visit his church immediately if he made it home alive. "I drove one of Bob's trucks, along with some of the crew from the *Sea Star*, back up to Marblehead, where I'd left my car at Bob's house, then I drove on to Danvers. The first thing I did was walk to church. As I was walking, somebody driving by pulled up alongside me and just stared at me like he saw a ghost. Then he shouted, 'Sarge! It's you—everybody up here thinks you drowned.' Apparently the storm had not only made the local news but also the national news, because later, when I called my mother, she told me she was worried sick, she had heard about the surprise storm on the news and knew that men died out at Georges Bank. When I got to church I just sat there and thought about things and said, 'Thank you for my life.'"

Peter's day wasn't over yet, because he and his father had to go straight to the Boston Coast Guard command center and explain what happened. And so the two men climbed into Peter's truck and began the two-hour ride to Boston, saying very little. Like Ernie, Peter had gotten almost no sleep since he was awakened early Saturday morning more than two days ago.

Meanwhile, approximately two hundred miles out at sea, Ernie knew that the raft was leaking air at an ever-increasing pace. He moved from one valve to another, pumping the raft, with almost no time to rest in between. There was no longer much sense in rationing the cans of water because for the first time he felt that soon he would not be able to keep up with the leaks, and the raft would sink. Then the ocean would make quick work of him.

He drank a can of water, stuck his head out of the raft and searched the lonely horizon, then went back inside and began the pumping process. The salty seawater ate into the abrasions that crisscrossed his body. Sitting was agony but lying down was worse, and he tried to stretch his legs to stop the cramping, but moving his legs was becoming harder and harder. Part of his mind told him he was probably finished, that all his effort was for nothing. But the other part, almost a voice, reminded him to keep going, that today could be the day. A phrase from his days in the military popped into his head: "maximum use of available resources." He had stitched the door, tied patches over the valves, and controlled his intake of water and cookies. Now he turned his mind to rescue. He figured that besides the flares he needed some other movement to attract the attention of pilots, and decided he'd wave the orange survival bag outside the raft's door if a plane came. The sun had not broken through the cloud cover as Ernie had hoped, but the clouds appeared to be high up and a plane could fly below them. They gotta come today, he thought. I've done all I can.

The men in the P-3 craned their necks and scanned mile after mile of gray, rolling sea. This search was very different from their submarine patrols because they couldn't rely on any of their electronics except radar, which could find a boat but not a raft. If someone was in a life raft, the radar wouldn't pick it up, and the men wondered if they could spot a raft with the naked eye in such a huge expanse of ocean.

They had been flying the search grids for over an hour when radioman Craig Martin shouted that he saw something, something orange. The pilot banked the aircraft in the direction Martin pointed.

Ernie was close to what can only be described as a catatonic state. It was 9 a.m., and hypothermia had advanced to the point where he was somewhere between life and death, enduring each minute as it came. His entire body, not just his feet, was slowly going numb. Far off, he thought he heard a droning sound, and it took a couple seconds for the sound's meaning to register in his brain. *A plane!*

A jolt of adrenaline coursed through his frozen limbs, and he grabbed a flare, stuck it out the door, and fired. The red flare and trailing smoke arced high into the sky. He could see the plane off in the west. He forced his shaking, half-numb hands to clutch another flare and fired it off. The plane began a turn. Now it was heading in his direction. He thrust the survival bag out the door and waved frantically. The plane roared directly over him. Finally, Ernie's three long days of uncertainty had come to an end: he knew he had been seen.

Minutes later a second, smaller plane flew over Ernie and dropped a string of orange marker buoys and a radio. The radio fell too far from the raft for him to retrieve it, but one of the marker buoys drifted by the raft's door and Ernie grabbed it. Inside was a message: "If other crewmen aboard, wave."

The message only confirmed what Ernie had known all along, that his crewmates never got out of the *Fair Wind*. Ernie sat back. There was relief, but no jubilation at being found.

When the P-3 radioed back to Boston Coast Guard command headquarters that they had spotted a raft and that someone had waved an orange bag out the door, Bob Eccles was astounded. "Even though this is exactly what I'd been hoping for, I could hardly believe it. For a P-3 to spot a tiny life raft was just about miraculous." Eccles and the command center crew immediately notified the other planes involved in the search, as well as the cutter *Active,* which had been searching since it went to the aid of the *Sea Fever.* The *Active* was approximately three hours away from the raft, but it was the closest Coast Guard vessel to the raft.

Commander Carl Helman and Operations Officer Dave Nicholson immediately directed the cutter to the location where the raft was spotted, approximately thirty miles east of where the *Fair Wind* went down. (Ernie was at the southeasternmost end of Georges Bank, and would have been off the bank had it not been for the ballast bag, which acted like a drogue, or sea anchor, slowing the drift rate of the raft.) The radioman on the *Active* was able to raise a Japanese long-liner fishing vessel even closer to the raft than the cutter was, and he requested that they too steam toward the raft.

Family members were alerted that a raft with a person on board had been spotted and that the *Active* would be on the scene in three hours. Maria Pavlis, Billy Garnos's fiancée, remembers the roller coaster of emotions, and how her hopes soared, knowing the life raft on the *Fair Wind* could hold all four crewmembers. The press also learned about the sighting of the raft, and area newspapers, radio, and television began reporting and speculating about who might be inside. The *Cape Cod Times* reported that "a Navy reconnaissance plane spotted a lifeboat with at least one man on board that was believed to be from the *Fair Wind*. It was a covered lifeboat, which means that the entire crew might be on board." The crewmen aboard the *Active,* racing to the raft, also wondered who was inside, amazed that anyone could have survived both the storm and the harsh November nights.

About 12 p.m., Ernie looked out of the raft and saw a fishing vessel, about one hundred feet in length, approaching his raft. It was the Japanese long-liner, and when it was about two hundred yards from Ernie, it stopped and stood by. Ernie wondered why the vessel halted and no one came to get him. He waited several minutes, then waved the survival bag out the door to make sure they knew someone was alive inside. The boat still did not move. For a moment Ernie wondered if his hold on reality was faltering. He wasn't imagining this boat, and those on board clearly knew he was in the raft, but why weren't they coming?

Ernie didn't know that the Coast Guard had asked the fishing vessel to stand by but not attempt a rescue because the *Active* was on the way. The Coast Guard didn't want to take any chances now, as the Japanese ship did not have a small boat to launch nor was it clear if any medical personnel were aboard the fishing boat.

After forty-eight hours in the ocean or in the raft, Ernie knew he could hang on awhile longer. Even in his frozen stupor it was clear the fishing boat was not going to come any closer, so Ernie figured a Coast Guard helicopter or cutter would arrive soon. He sat back inside his floating igloo, continued to pump the air chambers, and dreamed about sleeping in a warm bed.

He waited for an entire hour until he heard the sounds of another ship, and this time when he looked out, he saw the white hull and the red diagonal stripe of the cutter *Active*. Help was just minutes away.

CHAPTER 26

Salvation

THE FIRST STREAKS OF BLUE APPEARED BETWEEN THE cracks of the breaking cloud cover as men aboard the *Active* trained their binoculars on an orange speck off their starboard side. The Givens life raft bobbed easily on the swells, but even with the aid of binoculars the Coasties saw no signs of life on it. Wayne Hennessy began to think the P-3 pilots had been mistaken about having spotted one or more survivors because no one from the raft now waved or poked their head out the door. Tommy Dutton assumed it would be all or nothing: either all four men from the *Fair Wind* would be inside or nobody would be inside, and it was beginning to look like nobody.

Meanwhile, four young Coasties, including Tom McKenzie, readied the 26-foot motor lifeboat. The small launch, with a white hull and flesh-colored interior, looked similar to a dory, except it had a steering wheel in the middle toward the port side. Once the boat was lowered into the water and the cables were unfastened, McKenzie stood at the wheel, started the motor, and sped off toward the orange speck in the distance. "The surface of the sea was calm," says McKenzie, "but there were large rolling swells, spaced well apart at two-hundred-foot intervals. We were pretty anxious as we approached the raft because we didn't know what we'd find. Would the raft be empty or would all four crewmembers from the *Fair Wind* be inside? We also worried we might find them all dead."

McKenzie and crew were dressed in orange survival suits and their heads were protected and covered by white helmets. As the launch pulled within forty feet of the raft, there was still no sign of life inside, and McKenzie began to think the worst. When the launch was just a boat length away, McKenzie was startled by an incredible sight: the raft door parted and a head appeared. *"Oh, my God . . ."* whispered McKenzie.

"I'll never forget that moment," recalls McKenzie, "because his skin was blue. His chest was blue, his arms were blue, and his face and neck were blue."

The men with binoculars on the cutter watched in amazement. They too could see the blue face and bare blue chest of the man in the raft. Dave Nicholson recalls thinking that if the *Active* hadn't arrived exactly when it did, the man would have been dead within a couple of hours.

McKenzie eased the small boat a bit closer to the raft. "Beneath this big bushy beard I saw this man smile. I simply could not believe he could smile after what he must have endured. I shouted to him, 'You're going to be OK now, you've made it!' "

McKenzie's side of the boat, the port side, was abreast of the raft and McKenzie reached out and held the raft while the other three crewmembers carefully pulled Ernie into their boat. As they wrapped him in several layers of brown blankets, McKenzie asked, "You're from the *Fair Wind*?" After Ernie nodded, McKenzie asked a second question. "Could anyone else from your boat still be alive?" Ernie shook his head.

The crew sat the lone survivor down on the forward bench, and one crewmember sat next to him, keeping his arm around Ernie's shoulder to make sure he didn't fall over. Then McKenzie turned the boat and raced back to the *Active,* hoping to get his passenger to a medical corpsman as quickly as possible.

Ernie felt like he might collapse as he sat freezing in the blankets. Sleep, not warmth, had become his greatest need, and he let his head drop so that his chin rested on the blankets covering his chest. It was now approximately 1 p.m., and the wool blankets were the first dry material he had felt in almost fifty hours.

As the launch pulled alongside the *Active,* McKenzie stood at the wheel, another man stood at the bow, a third stood ready at the stern. The crew then lowered orange bumper balls over the side of the launch next to the cutter. Ernie sat unmoving, huddled in the bow, where the fourth crewmember kept a protective arm around him, telling him everything was going to be all right. The launch pulled up alongside the cutter and the men on the cutter lowered a line, which the boat men hooked to their bow. Now the launch was being towed alongside the *Active* at the exact same speed. McKenzie kept his hands on the wheel to use the rudder so the launch would ride a few feet from the ship. Ernie never looked up at the ship. His whole body felt as if it was entombed in a block of ice. And now that he was saved, exhaustion swept over him, and he was barely able to stay awake. All he could think about was a dry bed, and sleeping for days.

Two large "boat falls" were lowered from the *Active* and McKenzie's crew tied one forward and one aft. Then the skipper brought the launch in tight against the ship. As the crew of the *Active* began hoisting the launch up to the main deck, helping hands reached out from the ship for the blue-colored man with the black beard. Ernie raised his head a bit and mustered enough energy to slide along the bench toward the ship. Then he extended both arms. Two crewmembers from the launch stood in the boat and supported Ernie as he forced himself to stand for the first time since the pitch-poling. With two men in the launch and three on the cutter all holding or supporting Ernie, they assisted him as he stepped over the cutter's rail and onto the main deck. McKenzie then had the launch lowered again and he raced off to retrieve the raft, so it could be analyzed and also so that no other search planes or vessels would mistake it for a second life raft.

One of the blankets covering Ernie parted and crewmembers on the cutter could see that Ernie didn't have even a T-shirt on. Wayne Hennessy remembers that the castaway looked like a mass of blue and reddish flesh that could barely move. "He was in bad shape, and I really felt for him. He was covered in abrasions and his lips were a dark purple." Radioman Bill Gatter concurred, adding, "It was nothing short of a miracle he was alive. His flesh was blue, his joints were swollen, and he really couldn't walk."

A stretcher was waiting, and the corpsman—who had training similar to that of an emergency medical technician—immediately had Ernie lie down. He knew the survivor was not yet out of the woods. The corpsman worried that because of poor blood circulation Ernie could still go into shock, and he wanted him in the prone position to keep his blood pressure up. Additionally, the corpsman knew Ernie was susceptible to heart attack until his core temperature returned to normal. Any extra movement by Ernie could lead to a quick death, because the sudden circulation could bring the cold blood from the outer limbs rushing toward the heart, stopping it—literally—cold. This was a critical point for a hypothermic victim, but Ernie felt nothing but relief to be away from the perpetual rocking motion of the raft and among fellow human beings who genuinely cared about his safety.

The corpsman and crew carefully lifted the stretcher and carried Ernie inside the ship to the officers room. They helped him slowly change into dry clothes, rewrapped him in blankets, and the corpsman took his vital signs. Then the corpsman placed a small bowl of soup before Ernie. Although Ernie had eaten cookies and drunk water on the raft, the soup was beyond description, not because of its taste but because of its warmth. He savored each mouthful, as a good number of the ship's crew silently watched. It was as if they were witnessing a man rise from the dead, and they didn't want to miss a single moment. When Ernie finished the soup, Dave Nicholson debriefed him and asked about the possibility of the rest of the crew being alive. "I remember thinking," says Nicholson, "here's this guy who has just gone through something absolutely terrible and now I'm going to start asking him questions. But I had to know if the others from his boat had the potential to be alive. When I started talking to him I was amazed at how coherent he was. He made it clear to us that he stayed with the overturned hull for at least forty-five minutes until it started to sink, and no one else got out. I asked him if the other crewmembers had survival suits on, and he answered, 'No time. It all happened so quickly. It was just luck I got out.'"

Meanwhile, Tom McKenzie had returned to the ship with the life raft in tow. McKenzie went inside to see how Ernie was doing, but the corpsman had already assisted Ernie to an officer's bed, where Ernie fell fast asleep. The corpsman remained worried. Ernie's feet appeared to be frostbitten and swollen to almost twice their normal size, and the corpsman was still concerned about shock or heart attack and the limited medical facilities aboard the cutter. The medic consulted with Captain Helman and Nicholson, and recommended Ernie be airlifted off the boat and flown directly to a hospital. The officers agreed, and radioed Boston operations center to request a helicopter, then started steaming west. Meanwhile, they let Ernie sleep.

*   *   *

Word spread among the fishing community that one crewmember of the *Fair Wind* had been found alive, but his name had not yet been released. Wholesale lobsterman Frank Collins remembers thinking, I'll bet it's Ernie. "I'd gotten to know Ernie," recalls Frank, "the same as I would any deckhand on a boat we unloaded, because the process took three or four hours. Ernie struck me as the kind of person who would be thinking, How am I going to get out of this predicament, rather than being in shock from what happened. He just seemed to have this mental toughness about him."

CHAPTER 27

The Airlift

PILOTS BUCK BALEY AND JOE TOUZIN WERE ONCE again at the controls of their H-3 helicopter. The last four days had been grueling between the many Maydays on Saturday, the flight to the *Sea Fever* on Saturday night, and the search for the *Fair Wind* on the western end of Georges Bank on Sunday. Now, on Monday afternoon, they were headed back out to the Bank, only this time it was to pick up survivor Ernie Hazard.

Baley remembers thinking how incredible it was that Ernie had been found alive. "We used some very specific charts and calculations to plan, conduct, and evaluate the success of searches. The Probability of Detection, POD, is one calculation that helps us determine how effective a given search is. Given the conditions we had been searching for Mr. Hazard in, I figured we had about a six percent chance of finding him, and that assumed we were looking in an area where he actually was. It was extremely gratifying to hear that he 'beat the odds,' and I thought if I were him, I'd go right out and buy a lottery ticket."

During the flight to Georges Bank the pilots were told to make a stop at Nantucket to pick up emergency medical technician Linda True of the Nantucket Fire Department. "I found out about the situation," says True, "when the fire chief rushed into my work area and said, 'Quick, we gotta go, the Coast Guard needs you.' We hopped in the chief's car and headed to the Coast Guard station, so I figured I was going to be put on one of the Coast Guard patrol boats and brought to the injured man. When I got to the station they took me to the men's room, handed me a dry suit, and said, 'Put this on.' Then the chief took me back to his car, and I said, 'What's going on here, aren't I getting on a boat?' And he said, 'Nope, a helicopter is picking you up and taking you out.'

"Thank God it was a beautiful, clear day because I'd never been in a helicopter. I sat between the pilot and copilot, and to the rear of us was the basket operator. When we took off I thought the helicopter would go straight up, but I was surprised how it went down the runway, slowly lifting. They put a headset on me, and they talked, probably to make me feel at ease, which I was."

Back on board the *Active,* Nicholson knew he would have to wake Ernie, but he was reluctant to do so. "I knew he needed more medical care than we could give him, but I also could see that because of the big ocean swells, the helo wasn't going to be able to land safely on the cutter. Instead the survivor would have to be lifted by basket. Being lifted by a cable into the air is no picnic, and I was worried this might really put him in shock!"

The crewman who had walked Ernie down to his sleeping quarters also felt bad about waking him up. He had listened to Ernie say all he needed was sleep and he'd be fine. The Coastie was also impressed that Ernie had kept his sense of humor. On the way to the room they passed through another room where the floor had been recently waxed. Each time the ship took a wave the furniture in the room slid to the opposite side, and the young Coastie said, "If you think this is bad, you should have been here yesterday." Ernie deadpanned back, "I would have liked that very much."

No one wanted to wake Ernie, but the corpsman finally did so, and as expected Ernie was not happy, and he especially did not want to be airlifted off the boat. After spending more than two days on the open ocean Ernie wasn't wild about being lashed into a basket supported by a single cable, then suspended above the seas he had so recently escaped. The corpsman sent for Tom McKenzie to help calm his "patient" and escort him up to the flight deck.

"I remember," says McKenzie, "he was really pissed off about being forced to leave. He said something like 'I was just feeling better and just getting warm and now you're going to put me in a basket dangling above the ocean. That makes no sense.'

"There really wasn't much I could say," recalls McKenzie, "and I could certainly understand why he was mad. Imagine you just got out of the freezing cold ocean where you hadn't slept in three days, and just as you're finally starting to rest, now we are going to put you in another scary situation. He was probably thinking, I survived all of this only to risk getting killed by a basket dangling by a cable one hundred feet above the sea and ship."

Adding to Ernie's sour mood was a lifelong fear of heights. Now was not the time, he thought, to test his anxiety with a ride at the end of a swinging cable. McKenzie, however, informed him that he had no choice, and the two men headed up the stairs to the flight deck, where Ernie was given a coat and a life preserver.

Ernie shook his head in disgust. How ironic, he thought, now that I'm safely aboard a ship, I'm being given a life jacket. Then he heard the far-off drone of the helicopter and looked up to see it coming out of the western horizon.

Through the windshield, Linda True could see the *Active's*

white hull getting closer with each second. "When we got to the cutter I couldn't believe how big the waves were—the cutter was just going way up and then pounding back down. The man in the back started to get the basket ready and I said, 'You're not going to put me in that! You better bring that injured man to me.' That cutter was bouncing up and down so much there was no way I was going to get in that tiny basket. The pilot said, 'Don't worry, we're going to lower the basket and then bring the man up.' I got my gear ready and went in the back of the helicopter and waited for the injured man."

The cutter was turned so that it rode into the wind and the helicopter turned in the same direction, approaching the ship from the stern. When Baley and Touzin had the helo at the appropriate height, they radioed the ship that they were ready and were lowering the basket. The basket was just large enough for Ernie to sit in, and the corpsman and McKenzie helped Ernie inside, wrapping him in blankets. There was no chance for McKenzie to wish Ernie luck, so deafening was the roar from the helicopter. The corpsman signaled to the hoist operator that all was ready, and Ernie held on for dear life as the basket swung up and off the cutter's deck. Ernie held the basket bars as tightly as he had the raft's inner straps during the height of the storm. He could see the cutter receding below him, and from above he was blasted by the turbulence of the whirling helicopter blades. Ernie did not look up until he heard the metal clanging noise of the basket hitting the door of the helicopter. The hoist operator grabbed hold of the basket and guided it inside the door and Ernie felt the basket rest on the floor of the helicopter. The thundering rotors drowned out any chance for talking, but Ernie was in no mood anyway, especially with the helicopter's door wide open, causing him to feel vertigo and disorientation. He wanted to get as far into the helo as possible, and the hoist operator and Linda True helped him out of the basket and into a prone position.

"I put a pair of headsets on Ernie," says Linda, "so that we could communicate. I explained we were going to Cape Cod, and then he would be transferred to another helicopter and brought to a hospital in Beverly or Salem. His face and hands were really cold, and his feet were bright red and felt like ice. The captain of the cutter had radioed us about how he'd been in the raft for about forty-eight hours and how he was wet the whole time. I wondered how anyone could have survived. I checked his vital signs and he was OK, and he was coherent, answering my questions with a word or two. I knew they had warmed him up on the cutter and he'd had some soup, so perhaps the cold temperature of his extremities was primarily from being in the basket, although the feet were in bad shape probably due to lack of blood circulation. My primary concern was that he'd go into shock, because that sometimes happens a little while after the trauma. I was also concerned about cardiac arrest. Every couple minutes I'd ask him how he was feeling and he always said fine. It was amazing that he never said a word about the discomfort he must have been in. We were flying to the mainland, and just before we got there I finally got him to talk a little more. He said, 'I'm OK, but I lost my buddies . . . they never had a chance.' I can remember thinking this is one brave man."

When the helicopter landed at Beverly Airport a crowd had gathered. Among them were the loved ones of the missing crewmen, Ernie's brother and a friend, and the media. As Ernie was carried in a stretcher from the chopper to a waiting ambulance, reporters and photographers jostled one another for a closer look at the "survivor." Ernie shrank from the lights of the television cameramen and ignored the shouted questions of reporters. Just as he was placed in the ambulance, a newspaper photographer stuck his lens toward Ernie's face and snapped away. Ernie's brother Brent and neighbor Ron Michalak shooed the intruder away and climbed into the ambulance to accompany Ernie to the hospital.

Newspaper accounts of Ernie's ordeal appeared within hours. The *Salem Evening News* chronicled how "relatives of the missing crewmen were at the airport looking for a ray of hope." The *Boston Herald* ran a story with photos summarizing Ernie's condition. "Hazard was 'in shock' and spoke little, according to close friend and neighbor Ron Michalak, who accompanied the ambulance to Beverly Hospital. Michalak said he 'cried for ten minutes' when he heard Hazard was alive this morning, and held on to his friend's hands. It was the only communication necessary. 'Ernie is a pretty rugged kid,' Michalak said. 'He has a love for the sea. He eats, sleeps and drinks lobster fishing.' Michalak's wife, Marilyn, said Hazard is like 'an uncle' to her children. 'You would not believe how many people love that man,' she said." The story also included the following quote from Ron Michalak: "If I had to put money on somebody in a spot like that, it would be Ernie."

CHAPTER 28

A Different Kind
of Pain

THE DOCTORS AT BEVERLY HOSPITAL WHO EXAMINED Ernie found him to be in remarkably good physical condition considering that he had spent more than forty-eight hours either on or in the ocean in late November. They found that frostbite had affected both his thighs, where his flesh and tissue had actually frozen. Now the thawed skin was red and painful. His swollen feet, surprisingly, showed no signs of frostbite but instead he was diagnosed with a condition known as immersion foot, a nonfreezing injury occurring after the foot is submerged in water for a long period of time. The malady is less severe than frostbite because the tissue never actually freezes, and, ironically, Ernie's long immersion may have spared his feet from frostbite. Still, the immersion foot syndrome (similar to trench foot, found among soldiers exposed to damp conditions) can lead to nerve and muscle damage, joint immobility, infection, and even gangrene in severe cases. Ernie's discolored feet now gave him a constant aching discomfort—even worse than when he was in the raft—but the medical prognosis was for a complete or almost complete recovery of his feet and thighs.

While the hospital labeled Ernie's physical condition as "good," his mental health was another matter. "He's very down," said hospital spokesman Jack Good. "He doesn't want to talk about it until he finds out about his shipmates." The truth of the matter was that Ernie didn't want to talk about what happened at all unless it was to one of his crewmates' loved ones. Inside, he knew Billy, Rob, and Dave were dead, but he couldn't bring himself to say those words just yet.

Maria Pavlis learned from Coast Guard spokesman Captain Clyde Robbins that the search for Billy and the rest of the crew would resume on Tuesday. Robbins, however, had debriefed Ernie, and was not optimistic that any other crewmembers had escaped the overturned *Fair Wind,* and he shared this assessment with the families. This came as no surprise to Maria. She felt she knew Billy was gone the minute she first learned that Ernie was the only one inside the raft.

On Tuesday, Maria decided to visit Ernie, wanting to give him comfort despite her own sorrow. She had spent the last two days with Billy's family, and when Billy's parents learned she was going to see Ernie, they too decided to go. "When we saw Ernie in that hospital bed," says Maria, "we all broke down and cried. Ernie barely talked, he just kept squeezing our hands. We were all too choked up to talk, and it was obvious Ernie was physically and emotionally drained. It was all so emotional. On the one hand, we knew Billy and the others were gone, but on the other hand, we were just so happy Ernie was safe and was going to be all right."

Ernie wanted to comfort Maria and Billy's parents, but what

could he say? The heartache he felt for them and for his lost crew was more extreme than his physical pain—even worse, in fact, than the terror he felt at the height of the storm. He was experiencing the first pangs of "survivor guilt."

Why did I make it, he wondered, when the others did not, and so much of my survival depended on luck? The question is a quite normal reaction to a traumatic event where others perish. However, the survivor doesn't feel anywhere close to normal, but rather depressed and in jeopardy of falling into an abyss from which he cannot climb out. This was a new challenge the accident flung at Ernie, and it was every bit as difficult to endure as the pounding of the seas and the trauma of hypothermia, frostbite, and immersion foot.

Ernie was overcome by two diametrically opposed emotions: gratitude for being alive and intense sorrow for the loss of his crewmates. In the raft, he had dreamed of a dry, warm bed, a steaming mug of coffee, and hours of uninterrupted sleep. Yet now that he had those things he simply could not allow himself to enjoy them fully. Instinctively, he knew that his ordeal was not over and he steeled himself to be buffeted by strange and dark emotions. Just as he had in the raft, he would have to ride this out.

While Ernie lay in his hospital bed on Tuesday, *Fair Wind* owner Charlie Raymond was high above Georges Bank in a Coast Guard plane. With him was George Berry (Dave's father) and Rob Thayer's uncle. Charlie scanned the ocean below with binoculars. Gone were the towering, cresting seas of the storm, replaced by an endless expanse of gray-green swells. Charlie knew it was a long shot that anyone would be found alive, but he had to look, remembering his own close call at Georges Bank when a Russian trawler's net had caught the *Fair Wind*'s anchor cable. The trawler pulled Charlie's vessel behind it so that it was literally surfing along backward, and about to capsize at any moment. Fortunately, the Russians soon realized what had happened and cut their engine just in time. Charlie knew how lucky he had been, and he was hoping luck had somehow also saved Billy, Rob, and Dave.

The plane that carried Charlie was joined in the search by several other Coast Guard planes, as well as a navy reconnaissance plane. Down below the cutter *Active* conducted its own surface search, following the drift pattern that Ernie's raft had defined. None of the planes or the cutter spotted so much as a shred of debris from the missing vessel. The hunt continued all day, but by evening everyone knew that the *Fair Wind* and its remaining crew lay somewhere on the ocean floor, and the Coast Guard called off the search.

Ernie was released from the hospital on Wednesday, and looked forward to resting at his mother's house. Recuperation, however, was hard to come by because the phones were ringing almost constantly. Besides the calls of concern from friends and family, the Hazard home was deluged with calls from the media requesting interviews with Ernie. When Ernie refused, some reporters called back with offers of money, and still Ernie declined. It was just too soon, and the last thing Ernie would do was profit from the deaths of his friends. But when family members of the deceased crewmen called to learn the particulars of the accident and the storm, Ernie patiently retold the story. By now he had described the *Fair Wind*'s pitch-poling and his ensuing struggle several times, beginning back when he first arrived on the deck of the *Active*. And each time he told the story, it seemed as if a little bit of his soul was taken in the telling. But Ernie felt an obligation to explain to family members what had happened, just as he felt compelled to attend each of his friends' memorial services.

At the services, Ernie met the family members of the deceased and patiently answered their questions while battling a sense of shame for being alive while their sons, husbands, or brothers were gone. He would explain that it was pure luck that he'd gotten out. He didn't tell them about the countless split-second decisions he had been forced to make. He also listened to some of the families venting their anger at the National Weather Service as details of the botched forecast and the malfunctioning weather buoys began to come to light.

CHAPTER 29

The Inquiry and
a Thank-you

A WEEK AFTER THE ACCIDENT, THE COAST GUARD launched its official investigation, and Ernie was summoned to district headquarters in Boston. His testimony filled several pages of the inquiry report, recounting the period from Friday, November 21, when the *Fair Wind* left Hyannis, through the morning of the storm and the pitch-poling, and continuing with his two days in the raft. In addition to Ernie's testimony, Bob Brown and Charlie Raymond were questioned. The inquiry also took a closer look at the National Weather Service's forecasting. In the report, the Coast Guard marine safety commander, Harvey Knuth, stated, "It appears from this [testimony] that there is a definite discrepancy between the forecast and even the reporting of what the winds were compared with what the actual conditions were, at least what Ernie recalls. So at this point what I would like to do is contact the National Weather

Service and give them an opportunity to testify regarding this discrepancy if they care to."

The National Weather Service responded by sending marine focal point meteorologist David Feit to testify. Feit had been working at the National Weather Service office located at Logan Airport in Boston, and he, along with fellow staff members, were responsible for issuing offshore marine forecasts that included the regions of the Gulf of Maine, Georges Bank, and south of Nova Scotia. The Coast Guard commander asked Feit to describe the information used to make a forecast, and Feit explained that besides obtaining on-scene information from ships in the region, "one of the main things we've been relying on over maybe the past five years or so have been buoys placed out there, including the one on Georges Bank. I have the coordinates in my file here. That one [the Georges Bank buoy] has not been operative for some months, similar to the one in the Gulf of Maine." Feit went on to explain that when the buoys are operative, "they're supposed to come in every hour minimum; it reports by the wave height, wind direction speed, and some other parameters that are reasonably important to us. The thing that has been out on this buoy [the one at Georges Bank] has been the wind direction speed, which would have come in on an hourly basis had it been there and it would have given us perhaps that much of a jump." Feit went on to say that the Gulf of Maine buoy had been retrieved in May and had not yet been replaced at the time of the storm.

The Coast Guard commander asked if Feit's office had made any effort to get these buoys back on line, and Feit answered that indeed they had, writing several letters to the National Weather Service Data Buoy Office "indicating we considered these buoys important input to our program and particularly with winter coming up we felt it was extremely important that they get these buoys in operation again."

Feit then voluntarily added, "I think there were certain inaccuracies in the forecast . . . the storm . . . did not go as far east as perhaps we expected. The intensity of the storm in terms of its pressure grading, which determines how fast the winds are going to be, was underestimated to some degree and the worse part of it was moved over [to the west at Georges Bank]. It's a question of accuracy and how well we can do given the science and the state of the science and the material and observations that are available to us."

As details of the Coast Guard inquiry were made public, some family members of the deceased concluded that the testimony confirmed that the weather report was inaccurate in part due to the faulty weather buoys, and they considered litigation. (Later these family members and their attorneys filed a lawsuit against the National Weather Service, the result of which made news across the country; see the epilogue.) Ernie, however, wanted no part in any lawsuit. He was emotionally drained, and he wasn't interested in any compensation, and he worried that whatever he said about the accident could be twisted by lawyers, and made to reflect poorly on Charlie Raymond or the *Fair Wind*. Ernie had told the story enough times and was well aware of the toll it was taking on him. He often felt that the months after the accident were as difficult as his fifty hours in the raft. Ernie removed himself from the controversy, and let his sense of gratitude guide his way.

About a month after the accident, Grant Moore was working down in the engine room of the *Broadbill*, which was docked in Fairhaven. He heard someone shout, "Is Grant Moore here?" Grant put down his greasy wrench, and as he climbed the stairs to the deck, he wondered who would be looking for him in the middle of winter. On deck Grant saw a man with a bushy black beard. The man introduced himself as Ernie Hazard. "I just wanted to come down," said Ernie, "and thank you for what you did out there."

Grant doesn't remember if they said much more after that. "But it always stayed with me," says Grant, "that this man took the time to find me and thank me."

Ernie made one more stop: he tracked down Jim Givens at his office in Rhode Island and personally thanked him for building the raft that saved his life. After that, he did his best to get on with his life, keeping his *Fair Wind* buddies forever in his heart.

EPILOGUE

SEA FEVER
—JOHN MASEFIELD

I must go down to the seas again, to the lonely sea and the sky,
And all I ask is a tall ship and star to steer her by,
And the wheel's kick and the wind's song and the white sail's
*   shaking,*
And a gray mist on the sea's face, and gray dawn breaking.

I must go down to the seas again, for the call of the running tide
Is a wild call and clear call that may not be denied;
And all I ask is a windy day with the white clouds flying,
And the flung spray and the blown spume, and the sea-gulls crying.

I must go down to the seas again, to the vagrant gypsy life,
To the gull's way and the whale's way, where the wind's like a
*   whetted knife;*
And all I ask is a merry yarn from a laughing fellow-rover,
And quiet sleep and a sweet dream when the long trick's over.

Overlooking the ocean in front of the Lobster Pound store in
the Manomet section of Plymouth, Massachusetts, a portion of

this poem is inscribed on a plaque fitted into a memorial stone in memory of Gary Brown. Honour Brown, Gary's wife, had the stone placed there. The poem was also read at Billy Garnos's service.

Ernie Hazard

After the accident Ernie took some time off. In the spring of 1981 he was looking for a peaceful environment to work in and he found it as a maintenance worker in a cemetery, of all places. "It was a beautiful place—rolling lawns, flowers, a lake. So for a few months I used equipment to dig graves and maintain the cemetery."

Later in 1981 Ernie left the cemetery job and drove out to California to visit friends in Carmel. He decided to stay in the area doing odd jobs until the lure of the sea called, and he hired as a deckhand on a fishing boat out of Monterey. Ernie did not feel any trepidation about returning to the sea, and he needed a steady paycheck. This vessel, the *Southern Bell*, was the same size as the *Fair Wind*, fifty feet, and made day trips about ten miles offshore fishing for black cod. "I later learned that the guy I replaced on the boat died at sea when he got tangled in the gear and dragged over. And about the same time I also lost one of my best friends at sea. He was in a skiff on a calm day and somehow it flipped over, and he drowned. I was beginning to wonder if it was somehow payback for me surviving the raft ride."

Ernie eventually left commercial fishing but stayed in California. Reflecting on the November 1980 storm, he thinks that the experience of the crew of the *Sea Fever* was no less difficult than his own. "I marveled how Peter and his crew kept that flooded boat afloat. No windshields, a damaged pilothouse, losing a man overboard—Peter sure had a lot on his plate."

One might think that spending more than forty-eight hours on the brink between life and death would cause radical changes in behavior, but for Ernie the change was more subtle. "There's no reason for me to be here, so I figure what the hell. Since the storm hit around Thanksgiving, I tend to think that's my real birthday, my second life. These are free years I'm living. And so I don't let little stuff get to me. And when bigger problems come along I figure I'll solve it somehow. Although I don't always make the best of these extra years, I am surely thankful for each and every day. Everyone involved in that storm is in my mind all the time, every day.

"My life has been incredible. I've met so many fascinating people—some important, some famous, and some just special. And I appreciate the little things. Each day I take the long way to work, just to see the beauty of the coast. It's hard to say if this appreciation is from the raft experience or just the way I am now . . . maybe a little of both."

When this writer asked Ernie if he thought God saved him because he had plans for him, Ernie joked, "I think God was too busy to take on my problems. Maybe I was spared to keep me out of his hair."

Nancy Antonich (Dave Berry's mother)

Nancy Antonich wrote to me after I first contacted her, and in her letter she commented, "I have a drawer which contains newspaper clippings, letters and other paraphernalia relating to David and the loss of the *Fair Wind*. It's been a long time since I've looked in that drawer, but I opened it up yesterday on a rainy day and memories came flooding back. His brothers and I still miss him every day of our lives."

Included with the letter from Nancy was a poem titled "Fishing," which Dave wrote when he was ten, which, in hindsight, is a bit haunting:

FISHING

Fishing is a lot of fun
You can go rain or sun
Whether off land or in a ship
Or on a little boat that will tip.

Buck Baley (helicopter pilot)

After his first Air Station Cape Cod tour, Buck was transferred to Scott Air Force Base in Belleville, Illinois, in 1983 to serve as the Coast Guard liaison to the Air Force Rescue and Recovery Service. In 1986 he returned to Air Station Cape Cod, where he once again flew H-3s, until 1999. This was followed by a position in the USCG District Office in Boston doing exercise and contingency planning as well as managing the Coast Guard Reserve Program throughout New England. His final assignment as a captain was in Washington, D.C., where he was the CG liaison to the Director of the Office of National Drug Control Policy at the White House. In 1998 he retired from active duty and now works at the Volpe National Transportation Systems Center in Cambridge, Massachusetts, as an information technology specialist.

Hugh Bishop (lobster fisherman)

Hugh Bishop still lives in Marblehead and has been fishing for sixty years. "In 1947, when I was ten years old, I went out lobster fishing for the first time with a longtime lobsterman in Marblehead. As dawn cracked that morning, something got into me which has never left, a lifelong fishing addiction. One thing led to another and, by 1974, after a couple of years of deliberation, I decided to follow my childhood friend and rival, Bob Brown, into offshore lobstering on the continental shelf. For years we had always tried to catch one more pound of fish or lobster than each other.

"By the end of 1979, I had decided to stop offshore lobstering because of an ominous feeling about fishing on the continental shelf in a fifty-foot vessel. I realized it was too small for the job. Then the *Fair Wind* was lost, and it affected me greatly.

"From 1980 to 2005, I fished the *Mistress* out of Gloucester and Marblehead as a line trawler. Feeling advancing years taking their toll, I sold the *Mistress* in the summer of 2005 to a younger fisherman friend in Gloucester, where she is now berthed at the State Pier. Ironically, not seventy-five feet away is berthed the *Sea Fever*."

Bradford Bowen (*Sea Fever* crewmember)

"It's hard to believe," says Brad, "that nearly three decades have gone by since the accident." Brad is still a commercial fisherman, now hailing from New Bedford, Massachusetts, fishing for groundfish during the winter months and lobster in the summer and fall. The challenges of going to sea still intrigue him, but Brad says that the stricter government regulations are sometimes tougher than the fishing itself.

Brad adds that there is still something awesome about the draw of being at sea. "To this day I sometimes tune in to the Boston traffic report while at sea, helping to remind me that instead of looking at a car's taillights, I'm treated to incredible sunrises and sunsets with porpoises swimming by the boat.

"Working on this book project has brought back memories that I have tried very hard to forget. It has made me feel lucky to tell my part of the story but at the same time guilty thinking of all the fishermen and mariners that don't get to tell theirs. Most significant to me, *Fatal Forecast* reminds me that I survived and was given a chance to marry my wife, Suzanne, and have the opportunity to raise three beautiful girls, Shelley, Meagan, and Jessica—the most important people in my life."

Peter Brown (captain of the *Sea Fever*)

Peter Brown has continued his career as a fisherman and lobster-man since the accident. In 1984 he was able to go into business for himself when he bought the *Sea Star* from his father, Bob. "That boat," says Peter, "was a seventy-foot steel-hulled lobster boat that was out that same terrible day in November 1980, but made it through the storm without incident. So I knew she was a good safe boat. I fished her until 1988, at which time I had my present boat built; she is named after my oldest daughter, Rachel Leah. The *Rachel Leah* is a much bigger boat than the *Sea Star* and would make the *Sea Fever* look like a small inshore lobster boat."

Peter says that since the storm he monitors a number of different weather forecasts and has a weather fax on board that gives him weather charts out of Halifax to get a different view of the ever-changing conditions out over the offshore waters. He's especially alert in the fall for the same weather scenario that occurred during his ordeal.

"I never want to see conditions like that again, never want to see a friend or a crewmember on my boat lost because of a bad forecast. Gary Brown was a good man, he certainly didn't do anything wrong which caused him to go over that day. He was just doing what he was told to do, what needed to be done. I liked fishing with Gary; he worked just as hard as I did and kept coming back for more. If he ever slowed up a bit, all you had to do was bet him you could do something faster or better and his competitive nature took over. I think of Gary a lot, fishing together and the good times which are my best memories of him, but even those great memories are always broken by the vivid image of him in the water just behind the boat in those huge waves. I can still see the look in his eyes. I'll never forget it."

Bob Eccles (Coast Guard lieutenant)

Bob retired from the Coast Guard in 1992 as a lieutenant commander, having served twenty years on active duty: sixteen years in the Coast Guard as a commissioned officer and four years in the navy as an enlisted man. "When I retired, I bought a thirty-three-foot sailing vessel, and for a year cruised up and down the East Coast between Nantucket and Key West. One day I pulled into Savannah, meaning to stay the weekend. I've lived here ever since." He then started a tour boat company focused on educating passengers about marine life, and although he has now sold the company, he continues to captain the boat part-time.

Bob summarizes his lasting memory of the storm as follows: "I'll always remember that storm because of the number of life-threatening calls we received at the operations center. We would be consumed by our efforts regarding one ongoing 'sinker,' and then we would be advised of another desperate call for help."

Carl Helman (commander of the *Active*)

"The USCGC *Active* was my first command in New England. Later I commanded the USCGC *Hamilton* out of Boston. I'm ninety-five percent retired now, doing a little consulting for Harris Corporation related to Coast Guard Operations, Organization and Communications. I keep busy with work around the home, golfing, fishing, traveling, and volunteering."

Referring to the many rescues and Maydays of the November storm, Carl says, "The event gave me greater respect for the life and difficulties that the New England fishermen face and their determination and dedication to provide for their families. Additionally, this storm instilled in me more respect for the type of hazardous weather that can quickly show up without warning in New England, a respect that served me well the rest of my career at sea in the Coast Guard. Those storms that come up the coast and explode on Georges Bank don't get named but they can be worse than a hurricane. Years later, when the storm that is now known as the Perfect Storm hit the area, I was chief commander of all the cutters in the Northeast. When the Perfect Storm hit, all I could think of was the storm of November 1980, and how similar they were."

Wayne Hennessy (quartermaster on the *Active*)

Retired from the Coast Guard in 2004, Wayne Hennessy now resides in Maine. "The patrol we did in November 1980 on the *Active* changed my perspectives about the Coast Guard and on life itself. We were excited about returning home after a long patrol in the Caribbean when the storm hit. Initially our cutter was diverted to several cases to rescue fishermen from their sinking boats, then the call came in to proceed offshore to Georges Bank, where we were put in charge of the search effort for the *Fair Wind*. Many of us were thinking, This is futile—nobody could survive in this cold water. We were quickly silenced when the raft was sighted and furthermore proven wrong when we saw the sole survivor being brought alongside the cutter by our small boat. We were humbled. Since then, when I was in charge of coordinating a search, I kept this case in the forefront of my thoughts—I did not want to be wrong again in my judgment."

Jim Leboeuf (lobster fisherman)

Jim still lives in the area of Massachusetts known as North Shore, and is now the owner of a seafood company. "When I was captain of the fishing vessel *Horizon* in 1974, Bill Garnos and David Berry were two of my crew. It was David's first offshore lobster venture and he loved every minute of it, as did Bill. Ultimately, it would end their lives much too quickly.

"It seems long ago that David's father, George, came to my door to tell me the *Fair Wind* was missing. Now I think back to the time I spent offshore and feel fortunate to have sailed with Bill and David. I often feel guilty about helping to start their fishing careers, but in my heart I know they would have gone anyway."

Tom McKenzie (*Active* crewmember)

Tom now lives in Barnstable, Massachusetts, and teaches at the Massachusetts Maritime Academy. "Seeing Ernie in that raft was a life-changing experience for me. I just marveled at how one person can fight to survive. He was a pure survivor, and I never forgot that. When you see, in person, how this man did not give up—even when there wasn't much hope—well, it really gives you inspiration."

Anthony Militello (captain of the *Hattie Rose*)

Anthony Militello, captain of the *Hattie Rose*, which sank off Cape Cod, remained a fisherman for ten more years after his harrowing ordeal, and now works for a freezer warehouse company in Gloucester, Massachusetts, where he lives. Militello explained that while he doesn't think about the accident often, he does get a flush of memories "when it's stormy out and especially in February when it happened. I now have no desires to go back fishing, and for a while I didn't care to go on my friends' speedboats."

Grant Moore (captain of the *Broadbill*)

"That November storm gave me a total new respect for nature and how quickly conditions can change. You can't help but be sobered by what we saw. Peter and I still fish the eastern edge of Georges Bank, but now we are in larger boats. Although the *Broadbill* was larger than the *Sea Fever* and *Fair Wind,* I realized even that wasn't big enough, and that was really driven home during the April Fool's storm of 1982. We were off the tip of Cape Cod when we were slammed by a rogue wave. We went up and over the wave and were then in a free fall. When we landed, water poured in the pilot-house door and down into the fo'castle. The boat went over on its side. More water poured in the starboard-side windows. The next thing I know, there's a fire in the light fixture. Without thinking I reached up and the electricity blew me across the pilothouse. We were able to get the fire out, and somehow get into Province-town without issuing a Mayday. All the electronics were gone on the boat. That's when I knew for sure that I had to get a bigger boat, and the one I fish on now is seventy-seven feet."

David Nicholson (operations officer on the *Active*)

Dave Nicholson went on to command three Coast Guard cutters and retired as a flag officer but says he'll never forget the day he helped rescue Ernie. "To look into the eyes of a man whose life you know at that instant you are saving, and he knows you are saving—not rescuing, but saving—is not unusual for Coast Guard men and women in helicopters and coastal stations. It is truly rare for those who sail in the largest cutters. I remember the look as though it happened today. An instant like that lasts a whole career, and I was thankful for being in a crew that was prepared and I carried that drive to be prepared in each cutter I sailed."

Maria Pavlis (Billy Garnos's fiancée)

Maria Pavlis lives in Massachusetts and has recently retired after thirty-nine years of teaching the second grade. She remembers how difficult the months were after Billy's death. "After visiting Ernie in the hospital I went back to my apartment, the apartment I shared with Billy, and the next few days were the longest of my life, especially Thanksgiving. I knew that if I stayed alone in our apartment I'd go crazy, so the next week I forced myself to go back to my job as a teacher. I may have been robotic in the classroom and just going through the motions, but looking back, I can see that was the wisest thing for me.

"I couldn't help but think how unfair things were. Billy had just started opening up to me about the combat he saw in Vietnam and I thought to myself, Didn't he go through enough? I remember canceling all our wedding plans, and thinking how Billy seemed so happy with his life and with the thought of our future together. Later when Charlie Raymond finished building the new boat, he had me christen it. It was called the *Michael and Kristen*. For me it was a bittersweet moment, but I appreciated Charlie not forgetting me or Billy. In fact, my heart broke for Charlie because he loved those men."

Now, twenty-six years after the sinking of the *Fair Wind,* Maria adds a perspective graced by time and wisdom. "This tragic event took Billy from me," says Maria, "but I was so blessed to have known him and loved him. I still wear the diamond he gave me. I never did get married. It just never happened. The crew on the *Fair Wind* were such brave young men lost on that November day. What a devastating loss to their families and friends. However, there was a miracle that emerged from this tragedy. Ernie Hazard was spared. It is unbelievable what he went through and how he fought to survive."

Richard "Sarge" Rowell (*Seafarer* crewmember)

After the accident Sarge made an old-fashioned baby cradle as a gift for Honour Brown, Gary's wife. This was Sarge's way of showing how much he thought of Gary. Despite the trauma of the storm, Sarge never felt any fear of the sea, just respect. "Within a week of the accident," says Sarge, "Peter and I were back out fishing. I never thought of quitting because this is how I made my living. I stayed fishing for the Browns for ten to twelve more years. I went out on the *Andrea Gail* and the *Hannah Bowdin* swordfishing several times, but I thought thirty to forty days at sea was a bit much. So when Peter purchased the *Sea Star* from his father and fished Georges Bank, I fished with him rather than with his father at the Grand Banks, because we stayed out five days rather than thirty. I really enjoyed my time with Pete—he became a great friend and teacher. I was given the opportunity to captain the *Sea Star* and Pete's newer boat, the *Rachel Leah.*

Looking back, those days fishing with the Browns were some of the most enjoyable times of my life.

"When I got married and started a family I wanted to be home more, so I purchased my own boat, a forty-two-foot wooden lobster boat, which I used to lobster-fish off Beverly, Marblehead, and Salem. About five years ago I bought my current boat, a thirty-eight-foot fiberglass boat which I named the *Allison Gail,* after my first daughter. Fishing closer to home was the right move for me because I got to coach my kids' softball and soccer teams and just see a heck of a lot more of my family.

"In twenty-seven years of fishing, I've never experienced waves the size of the ones in the November storm, nor have I seen a storm explode so fast. Maybe one reason I didn't leave the fishing business after the accident is because I truly enjoyed my work. I've seen other guys who are in it just for the money and they don't last long."

Linda True (emergency medical technician)

Linda True still lives on Nantucket, although she is no longer an emergency medical technician. "EMTs often ask themselves over and over what ever happened to a person they responded to—did they make it or not? Well, Mr. Hazard was one of those people that was always in the back of my mind. Did he survive? Did he have any physical impairments? Is he still fishing? So it was gratifying to learn, after all these years, that Mr. Hazard did make it and is doing fine."

The Court Case:
Honour Brown et al. vs. U.S.
(Civil Action number 81–168-T)

Some of the families of the deceased (Garnos, Berry, and G. Brown) filed a lawsuit charging the National Weather Service with negligence and asking $3.2 million in damages. After a seven-day, nonjury trial in May 1984, U.S. District Court Judge Arthur Tauro ruled for the plaintiffs that the federal government was liable and he awarded the families $1.2 million in damages. This was the first time in the history of the United States that the government (National Weather Service) was found responsible for an inaccurate forecast. Judge Tauro said government negligence in issuing the forecast was a "substantial factor" in the deaths of the fishermen. The ruling was featured in newspapers across the country and spawned articles both for and against the decision, many with simplistic but eye-catching headlines such as "Weatherman Is Found Guilty." The lawsuit, however, was quite complex and at its heart was the government's failure to repair or replace the malfunctioning weather buoys. (To read selected testimony from the court case, see the author's Web site: www.michaeltougias.com.)

The ruling, however, did not stand for long. In 1986 the U.S. First Circuit Court of Appeals reversed the judgment, holding that the government was protected from liability "because the decision to issue a weather forecast without repairing the buoy was the result of the exercise of discretion within the meaning of the discretionary function exception of tort liability." In other words, the government is protected from liability because the act of weather forecasting is a discretionary function for which the U.S. government cannot be held liable as outlined in the Federal Tort Claims Act.

AUTHOR'S NOTE

If I'm going to devote two or three years to researching and writing a story, the event has got to grab me, shake me, and ultimately make me so curious that I just can't let go. But having a burning interest isn't enough—the people related to the event have to be open, honest, and kind enough to carefully answer my questions. And so I felt lucky that the first person I contacted was Sarge (Richard Rowell). I called Sarge first simply because he was the only one of the survivors I could find when searching an online directory for Massachusetts. After I explained why I was calling I waited for his response, knowing it could be guarded, vague, or even curt. Instead we immediately fell into a comfortable conversation, and with that first phone call I was off and running.

I explained to Sarge that I had come across the story of the *Sea Fever* and the *Fair Wind* while skimming through Coast Guard marine casualty reports during my research for *Ten Hours Until Dawn* and asked him if he thought he could help me track down the other men. Sarge said he could definitely put me in touch with Brad and Peter, but he didn't know what had happened to Ernie Hazard. I felt a little of the wind go out of my sails, knowing that without Ernie there could be no book. Then Sarge said that if anyone knew what happened to Ernie it would be the owner of the *Fair Wind,* Charlie Raymond. Sarge gave me Charlie Raymond's phone number and encouraged me to call him.

Sure enough Charlie was helpful, and said that although he had not seen Ernie in years, he thought that Ernie had moved to California. I quickly found Ernie's telephone number, but before calling, I tracked down additional information about the event. I first went through various 1980 editions of local newspapers, reading about the storm, the boats involved, and how the Coast Guard responded to so many Maydays. There were a few good articles, but a week later I found an excellent story about the event, published in *Yankee* magazine and written by Evan McLeod Wylie. These write-ups, in addition to the marine casualty report, gave me a good overview of what had transpired out at Georges Bank, and I now felt I could at least call Ernie and be conversant with some of the details.

A week later I spoke to Ernie on a Sunday afternoon, explaining that I found his story absolutely amazing and thought it needed to be told in its entirety. I asked him a few questions, and after just five minutes of talking I knew he was just the kind of man I wanted to work with. No pretense, no ego, just a directness that I found refreshing. I told him about the little bit of research I'd done, and explained that I wanted to fly out to California and interview him in person. He said sure. We decided I'd visit in three months, in May. In the meantime, Ernie did me a huge favor by mailing me a thick package of information about the accident and his survival. The material ranged from his handwritten account to the Coast Guard to an article in a 1982 edition of *People* magazine regarding Jim Givens and the life raft he created.

When May came, I called Ernie to find out what days were best to visit. He invited me to stay at his house, and I took him up on his offer. I figured we'd need at least two or three days to go over all the material, and I decided to spend almost a full week in California. I'm glad I did. I had one of the most interesting weeks of my life.

I conducted the interview with Ernie in a marathon session starting the evening of my first day and then continuing through the next two days. How this man sat so patiently and answered all my questions was in itself a minor miracle. When we were through, I felt like I'd been a fellow crewman aboard the *Fair Wind*. Ernie's explanations were so complete, I felt I had everything I needed. We celebrated with a few beers.

When I returned to Massachusetts I tracked down Grant Moore and interviewed him in the pilothouse of his 80-foot lobster boat, docked in Fairhaven, Massachusetts. Then over the next couple of months I conducted individual interviews with Sarge, Peter Brown, and Brad Bowen. Just like Ernie, they never tried to make themselves sound brave or felt the need to embellish. Equally important, each man's memories of the events matched the others'. To be sure, they felt different emotions at different times, and each had his own perspective in hindsight, but their recollection of a myriad of facts all matched perfectly. The other trait they had in common was that the men were all bright and articulate—which is often at odds with the way the public perceives fishermen. But to operate as successful captains, own your own vessel, and make a good living at something as dangerous and unpredictable as commercial fishing, you have to be tough, adaptable, and above all smart. This made my job so much easier.

After I talked with these key people I took a break from the interviewing process and focused on the wealth of information that was chronicled in the depositions and testimony during the lawsuit against the National Weather Service. I found this material at the National Archives in Waltham, Massachusetts. I wasn't looking for any blockbuster piece of information because I'd already talked to the men who had lived through the experience, but the files still yielded useful pieces of the story's mosaic, and in some cases let me hear the voices of people I could not interview, such as the testimony of Bob Brown when he was interviewed by the Coast Guard.

After exhausting the National Archives I turned my attention to the men and women from the Coast Guard who were involved in the storm. Locating the two senior officers of the cutter *Active,* Carl Helman and Dave Nicholson, was relatively easy, and they quickly brought me up to speed about the rescue of the *Determined* and their subsequent mission out to Georges Bank. I also had the good fortune to locate Wayne Hennessy, who served on the *Active* during the storm. Besides taking photos of Ernie's rescue, Wayne had kept in touch with many Coasties on the *Active* who remembered the search and the storm. My next two Coast Guard interviews were with the pilot and copilot of the helicopter that made the dangerous flight into the storm to assist the *Sea Fever.* Buck Baley and Joe Touzin patiently walked me through their activities during the flight and explained what they were thinking and feeling during the nighttime mission.

Of all the meetings I had with people involved in the story, my evening with Maria Pavlis was one of the most memorable. Charming and thoughtful, she gave the story a different perspective, of what it was like to be back on land and hearing— in agonizing bits of news—about the tragedy that had unfolded offshore.

Others who gave freely of their time and knowledge included Hugh Bishop, Nancy Antonich, Ted Bowen, Frank Collins, Tony Davern, Charlie Dutton, Bob Eccles, Jim Kendall, Jim Leboeuf, Tom McKenzie, Anthony Militello, Mike Sosnowski, Frank Sholds, Linda True, and Captain William Russ Webster. And there were many others who may have added only a single descriptive detail or two, but the cumulative effect of these kind souls gives the book a deeper richness, and to them I say thank you.

Many friends took a look at the first draft of *Fatal Forecast* and helped to make this a better book by offering their insights, including Adam Gamble, Bill and Kathleen Noren, Linda Walsh, my brother Mark Tougias, Frank Quirk III, super agent Ed Knappman. I would also like to thank editors Karen Thompson and Colin Harrison for their inspiration and many improvements to the manuscript.

Researching the ordeal the men of the *Fair Wind* and *Sea Fever* went through has not changed my love of the ocean, but it has increased my respect and wariness. I still go striped bass–fishing every chance I get and still take my kayak out to fish or ride the waves. In fact, my proximity to the ocean probably helped me write the book because I wrote the chapter about the pitch-poling of the *Fair Wind* and the blown windows of the *Sea Fever* when I was renting a cottage overlooking the ocean on Cape Cod in October. A two-day storm slammed the Cape while I was there, and between sessions of writing on my computer I waded out into the surf and cast for striped bass. The roar of the wind and the crashing of the waves were probably only 1 percent of the decibel level that assaulted Ernie, but it certainly helped me appreciate the sudden power and fury of the sea.

It was during that weeklong writing sojourn on Cape Cod that I reread my notes from my meeting with Ernie and tried to put myself in his place while he was in the raft, facing mountainous waves and extreme cold. The more I thought of what he endured, the decisions he made, and the steely outlook he developed, the more I realized how truly unique a human being he is. Ernie would disagree, of course, saying he was lucky and he did what anyone else would try to do, but I know better.

I like to think that when I undertook this book I had a big, blank white canvas in front of me, and the only way it could be painted was through interviewing the people involved with the storm. Each person contributed, painted his section of the canvas, and I was the lucky one who got to put my name on the bottom. But it's their painting, their story, and for their help I am forever grateful.

Be sure not to miss *The Finest Hours,* by Michael J. Tougias and Casey Sherman, another gripping true tale of adventure and rescue at sea, now available from Scribner in hardcover.

Turn the page for a preview of *The Finest Hours.* . . .

February 18, 1952

Captain Frederick Paetzel was not taking any chances with the storm that had overtaken his 503-foot oil tanker. Paetzel kept the Mercer's bow pointed into the rising seas, holding position, prepared to ride out the storm. The captain had guided the ship safely since leaving Norco, Louisiana, and now, just thirty miles southeast of Chatham, Massachusetts, he wasn't too far from his final destination of Portland, Maine. He might be delayed by the storm, but rough seas in the North Atlantic during the month of February were not unexpected, and he would bide his time until the storm blew itself out.

The nor'easter, however, showed no signs of weakening. Instead it intensified with each passing hour. By the time a pale hint of light indicated dawn's arrival, mountainous waves had grown to fifty and sixty feet and the wind approached hurricane strength, hurling a freezing mix of sleet and snow at the vessel. The Mercer took a terrible pounding yet rode the seas as well as could be expected, without any excess pitching or rolling.

Then, at 8 A.M., Captain Paetzel heard a sharp crack echo from the innards of his ship. He wasn't immediately sure what had happened, but soon the captain, along with several crew members, saw oil spewing over the ocean from the starboard side of the Mercer, and they knew the Mercer's hull had cracked.

The forty-eight-year-old captain immediately slowed the vessel's speed by a third and positioned the ship so that the waves were on the port bow, to keep the fracture from growing. After Paetzel alerted the rest of his crew about the emergency, he radioed the Coast Guard for assistance, reporting that his ship's seams had opened up in the vicinity of the number 5 cargo tank and its load of fuel was bleeding into the sea.

Once the Coast Guard was notified, Paetzel and his crew of forty-two men could only pray that the ship stayed together until Coast Guard cutters arrived. The German-born captain had been at sea since he was fourteen but he'd never seen a storm like the one he was caught in, nor had he ever heard the sickening crack of metal giving way to the sea.

Approximately 150 miles away, aboard the Coast Guard cutter *Eastwind,* radio operator Len Whitmore was doing his best to ignore the rolling motion of the ship and focus on the radio. A fishing vessel, the *Paolina,* out of New Bedford, Massachusetts, was overdue, and the cutter was involved in the search. The *Eastwind* was in the last known vicinity of the fishing boat, and Len repeatedly broadcast over the radio, hoping to make contact. Voice communication at the time was rudimentary and could only span about forty or fifty miles. Beyond that range, the only method of communication was Morse code, also known as CW, for Continuous Wave. Now Len was using his voice on the radio, hoping the *Paolina* was still afloat nearby, but his gut told him that the odds of finding the vessel were getting long as the storm continued to strengthen. . . .

Another Coast Guard vessel, the *Unimak,* which was also south of Nantucket searching for the *Paolina,* was diverted from that search and started pounding its way through the storm toward the *Mercer*. In Provincetown, Massachusetts, the cutter *Yakutat* was dispatched to the scene, as was the *McCulloch* out of Boston. . . .

Aboard the *Fort Mercer*, Captain Paetzel tensed each time a particularly large wind-whipped wave hit the vessel. Oil continued to stain the ocean, and the ship's quartermaster did his best to keep the bow into the oncoming seas. Paetzel had the crew don life vests, but beyond that safety measure, the crew could do little besides wait for the Coast Guard to arrive.

Remarkably, at 10 A.M., the *Boston Globe* was able to make a shore-to-ship telephone connection with the captain. Paetzel said the conditions were very rough and that waves had reached sixty-eight feet, rising up into the rigging, but he believed his ship "did not appear in any immediate danger." Still, he acknowledged he couldn't be sure because surveying the damage more closely from the deck would be suicidal. "We're just standing still," he added. As a final thought, he considered loved ones onshore and expressed a hope that "none of our wives hear about this." The *Mercer* was not listing, and since the earlier sound of metal splitting there had been no more serious events—Paetzel remained hopeful that the worst was behind them.

While Paetzel may have felt the *Mercer* was not in immediate jeopardy, he also knew the history of the partly prefabricated and welded T2 tankers, and that knowledge was not comforting. To date, eight of the tankers had been lost due to hull fractures, and they were particularly susceptible to cracking when large seas were accompanied by cold temperatures—the exact situation the *Mercer* was now enduring. The captain would breathe easier when the Coast Guard cutters were within sight.

Suddenly, at 10:30 A.M., another terrifying crack rang out, and the ship lurched. Paetzel instantly sent another message to the Coast Guard explaining that the situation was worsening. A cold sensation of dread coursed through the captain; he knew his ship might become the ninth T2 tanker to be taken by the sea.

The stress on the ship was now building, especially as one wave lifted the bow and another the stern, leaving no support in the middle. The storm had breached the tanker's welded hull, and the seas seemed intent on lengthening the crack. Captain Paetzel and crew were helpless to do anything other than wait for the cutters.

Another long hour went by without incident. Then at 11:40 A.M. a third loud report was heard as more metal cracked. Paetzel could now see the crack, extending from the starboard side number 5 cargo tank to several feet above the waterline, with oil spurting into the rampaging seas. At 11:58 A.M. Paetzel had another SOS sent, this one accompanied by the message "Our hull is splitting."

A couple of minutes later a wave smashed the tanker so hard that crewmen were thrown to the deck. When they got to their feet they couldn't believe what they saw: the vessel had split in two!

Crew member Alanson Winn said that when the final crack and split occurred it was so loud and violent he thought the ship had been rammed. "Then she lifted up out of the water like an elevator. She gave two jumps. And when she'd done that she tore away."

Paetzel was trapped on the bow with eight other men, while the stern held thirty-four crew members, and each end was drifting away from the other. Seas tossed the bow wildly about as if it were little more than a broken toy, first swinging sharply to starboard. The forward end of the bow rode high in the air, but the aft section sloped down to the sea, submerging a portion of the deck and washing away the lifeboats. Equally as devastating, the accident had knocked out the radio, and Paetzel could no longer work with the Coast Guard for rescue; nor could he offer instructions to the crew members on the stern. Paetzel and his men were helplessly trapped in the bridge—to leave might mean instant death. The bow wallowed in the monstrous seas, and without engine power it was broadside to the waves, taking direct hits.

The stern section, where the engine was located, was in much better shape, and all of it was above the seas. Right after the split, engineers immediately shut the engine down, but now the crew on the stern could see waves pushing the bow back toward them like a battering ram. Miraculously, the engineers were able to restart the engine. They put the propeller in reverse and were able to back the stern away before the bow ran them down. Their troubles, however, were just beginning. . . .

Through the long afternoon, Captain Paetzel and the men trapped in the bow huddled in the unheated chart room. Just after nightfall, the cutter *Yakatat* arrived at the scene, but the waves were too large for her to pull alongside the bow for a rescue, and the cutter hovered nearby, waiting for the wind and waves to ease.

On the bow of the *Mercer*, Captain Paetzel and crew were becoming desperate. The front of the bow section was sticking completely out of the water, but the aft section of the hulk, where he and his crew were trapped in the unheated chart room, was sinking lower into the sea. They were without any lights or other means to signal back to the *Yakutat*, and slowly the room was filling with water. Just before midnight they decided to try to move from the chart room to the forecastle room, where they hoped to escape the rising water and find signaling equipment. To do so, however, first meant somehow lowering themselves out of the chart room and onto the exposed deck, which was awash with spray, snow, and sometimes the sea itself. The door from the chart room to the deck was too close to the sinking end of the hulk, and the drop from a porthole to the deck was too great to risk jumping. And so the crew improvised, taking various signal flags and tying them together to create a line, which they lowered out the porthole on the forward side of the chart room. One by one the men started out, first lowering themselves down the signal flag line, then taking the most harrowing footsteps of their lives as they headed forward on the upward-sloping, icy catwalk.

The ship pitched and rolled, and the men ran toward the forecastle as seething white water surged around their feet. Radio operator John O'Reilly—who had been transmitting to Len Whitmore earlier that morning—slipped, lost his footing, and was swept overboard, disappearing into the churning abyss. The other eight crew members made it safely to the forecastle, including Captain Paetzel, who had been caught in his slippers when the tanker split, and made the crossing barefoot.

Captain Naab on the *Yakutat* had seen the men run across the catwalk, and he knew the tanker crewmen were desperate enough to do anything, so he decided he had better make another attempt to get them off. He maneuvered the cutter windward of the tanker. His men then tied several life rafts in a row, dropped them overboard, and let the wind carry them toward the tanker. Lights and life jackets were attached to each of the life rafts.

On the *Mercer's* bow, the survivors watched the rafts come toward them. It was decision time, and what an awful decision it was. Each man had to make a choice in the next minute that might mean the difference between life and death. There was no one to give them guidance, assurance, or even the odds they faced, because no one knew what would happen next. If they stayed with the fractured ship they risked the chance that she might roll over at any moment, taking them down with her, trapping them in freezing black water below. But to jump from the ship held its own perils, not the least of which was the possibility they would not land inside the raft. And if that happened they simply didn't know what the ocean would do to them. Maybe they would have the strength to swim to the raft and haul themselves up and in, or maybe the frigid seas would so weaken them that they would never even make it to the side of the raft, let alone climb aboard.

Three crew members on board felt the rafts were their best chance of escaping the storm alive. They crawled to the side of the deck and, one by one, threw themselves overboard and down toward the rafts. All three missed the rafts. The shock of the freezing water made swimming nearly impossible, and although they tried to get to the rafts, the mountainous seas buried them and they disappeared from view. Captain Naab watched in horror as the seas swallowed the men.

Suddenly one of the tanker crewmen, Jerome Higgins, still aboard the *Mercer*, saw how close the *Yakutat* was and made a fatal choice. He leaped over the rail, hit the water, and tried to swim to the cutter. In the howling darkness the seas swept him away and in a flash he was gone. Naab, not wanting to witness any more drowning, backed the cutter away and laid off, now knowing a nighttime rescue attempt would be suicidal for the tanker crew. The best option was to wait for dawn.

ABOUT THE AUTHOR

MICHAEL TOUGIAS is a versatile writer and the author and coauthor of eighteen books. In addition to *Fatal Forecast,* he is the author of *Ten Hours Until Dawn: The True Story of Heroism and Tragedy Aboard the* Can Do. This book was selected by the American Library Association as an Editors Choice, "one of the Top Books of the Year." Tougias and coauthor Casey Sherman teamed up and wrote a combination history/ocean rescue story titled *The Finest Hours: The True Story of the U.S. Coast Guard's Most Daring Sea Rescue.* This drama occurred in 1952 off the coast of Cape Cod when two oil tankers, in the grip of a nor'easter, were split in half and eighty-four lives were in jeopardy.

On a lighter note, Tougias's award winning humor book, *There's a Porcupine in My Outhouse: Misadventures of a Mountain Man Wannabe,* was selected by Independent Publisher as the best nature book of the year. The author has also written for more than two hundred different and diverse publications, including *The New York Times, Field & Stream, Fine Gardening,* and *The Boston Globe.*

Tougias has prepared slide lectures for all his books, including *Fatal Forecast,* and his lecture schedule is posted on his website at www.michaeltougias.com (interested organizations can contact him at michaeltougias@yahoo.com or P.O. Box 72, Norfolk, MA, 02056).

Through research into dozens of survival stories, Tougias has also prepared an inspirational lecture for businesses and organizations titled *Survival Lessons: Peak Performance under Pressure.* Tougias describes this presentation as "an uplifting way to learn some practical strategies and mind-sets for achieving difficult goals from those who have survived against all odds." He has given the presentation for all types of organizations, including General Dynamics, the Massachusetts School Library Association, NYU Surgeon's Roundtable, Lincoln Financial Services, Goodwin Proctor law firm, and many more. Interested organizations can contact him at michaeltougias@yahoo.com. For more details see www.michaeltougias.com.